M000119633

ALSO BY CHRIS ARTHUR

Irish Nocturnes
(The Davies Group, 1999)

Irish Willow
(The Davies Group, 2002)

Irish Haiku
(The Davies Group, 2005)

Irish Elegies
(Palgrave Macmillan, 2009)

Words of the Grey Wind
(Blackstaff Press, 2009)

On the Shoreline of Knowledge
(University of Iowa Press, 2012)

Reading Life
(Negative Capability Press, 2017)

Hummingbirds Between the Pages
(Ohio State University Press, 2018)

Hidden Cargoes

CHRIS ARTHUR

EASTOVER
— PRESS —

HIDDEN CARGOES

Chris Arthur

© 2022

ISBN 978-1-958094-03-7

ESSAYS

COVER & BOOK DESIGN — EK LARKEN

Versions of several of the essays in *Hidden Cargoes* have been previously published in the *Antigonish Review*, *Dalhousie Review*, *Fourth Genre*, *Hotel Amerika*, *ISLE: Interdisciplinary Studies in Literature and Environment*, *Montreal Review*, *New Hibernia Review*, *Terrain.org*, and *Water~Stone Review*.

Image accompanying Dedication is
Albrecht Dürer's *Hare*, 1502.

Image in "Particle Metaphysics" is
from the author's collection.

PUBLISHED IN THE UNITED STATES BY

EASTOVER
— PRESS —

www.EastOverPress.com

For Dorcas Sohn

Mad March Hare, artist, gardener,
owl rescuer, fairy godmother,
and so much more.

Your friendship, kindness, and
courage-in-adversity would need
another book to chronicle.
They've been an inspiration in
writing this one.

Hidden Cargoes is dedicated to you,
with love.

To pay attention,
this is our endless and proper work.

—MARY OLIVER, *OWLS AND OTHER FANTASIES*

Contents

Introduction

William Blake's famous lines urge us

> *To see a world in a grain of sand*
> *And a heaven in a wild flower,*
> *Hold infinity in the palm of your hand*
> *And eternity in an hour.*

This book challenges those who dismiss Blake as a dreamer or a madman. For them, sand grains are just sand grains, wildflowers no more than simple blooms. They believe that our hands can enclose nothing greater than what fits neatly in our grip, and that an hour is always confined within the palisade of its temporal duration. I leave to visionary geniuses like Blake the task of seeing on a scale that reveals worlds, heavens, infinity, and eternity. My aim is more modest. My essays try to strip routine's dulling insulation from the wires of experience so that the voltage of what's there can touch us, make us aware of the hidden cargoes that are held in such abundance in the unlikeliest of places—a girl's ear, a cigarette box, the letters of the alphabet, an owl's skull, a sprig of witchhazel. However much we contrive not to notice it, the electricity of wonder runs through everything. The twelve exercises in paying attention that constitute this book try to make that electricity more evident.

At the start of *Portrait Inside My Head*, Phillip Lopate provides an introduction that's subtitled "In Defense of the Miscellaneous Essay Collection." Since *Hidden Cargoes* is such a collection, should I likewise start by defending it?

Perhaps.

But such a tactic risks undermining what it's meant to support. Faced with an opening salvo of authorial defense, readers may suspect that what they're about to embark on lacks legitimacy. Why would it need to be defended unless its status was dubious?

I can see why almost any book might be thought to require an opening apologia. In a world in which so many people live in terrible need, the time and resources claimed by writing and reading might be thought questionable—frivolous, uncaring, selfish, irrelevant—unless a link can be demonstrated between them and some practical remedial upshot, a contribution to the common good. That apart, I see no reason why a collection of essays needs any more justification than a novel or a play or a book of poems.

In an essay about essays, provocatively titled "In Defense of Incoherence," E. J. Levy writes that "the form doesn't lend itself to mass market sales." But, she says, "that is precisely its charm and our pleasure in reading it." In her view, part of the appeal of this genre lies in the fact that it provides a "respite from the clamor of commerce." She urges essayists not to succumb to the pressure of making their work more palatable to the economic exigencies of publishing, particularly by presenting collections in a way that obscures the individual independence of each piece. To give the impression that essays can be subsumed beneath some organizing principle, to pretend there's an overarching structure according to whose linear blueprint they unfold, is to betray their essential nature. "The first impulse that brought us to the essay form," Levy reminds us, is art. And art is "not about the market or clever formal conceits, or even publication, but about wonder."

I hope what I've said doesn't swim against the current of Levy's argument. The idea of paying attention and, by so doing, seeing the hidden cargoes carried in the things around us, offers a loose commonality that links the essays I've assembled. But I wouldn't like it to be taken as a sign that I've surrendered to any kind of organizing principle. I join Levy in condemning such devices. The book's title and epigraph, and what I've said in this introduction, provide only the most general orientation. I've no desire to disguise the essentially miscellaneous nature of *Hidden Cargoes*. To invent some organizing principle that forces things into line, that gives the impression of a single narrative running unbroken from beginning to end, would be dishonest. The pages that follow don't dance to this tune. The essays are independently intelligible and can be read in any order—though I've tried to arrange them in a way that's in harmony with the music of their unfolding.

Some readers find this kind of collection an alarming prospect. They're suspicious of the absence of a point-by-point progression. They feel uneasy outside the safe anchorage provided by linearity, where everything conforms to a predictable pattern of unfolding. If such readers haven't fled the scene already, let me offer three reassuring touchstones—without, I hope, introducing the artificiality of the kind of organizing principle that Levy rightly condemns, or mounting a preemptive defense that might simply undermine what it seeks to foster.

First, as Graham Good puts it, "At heart, the essay is the voice of the individual." To the extent that an individual's voice reflects one particular personality, history, and worldview, *Hidden Cargoes* can claim that degree of homogeneity. Second, I agree with Levy about the fundamental nature of art. All of my essays share a common origin. They are rooted in moments of wonder. Third, in a comment that nicely catches the way in which single essays relate to a collection, Richard Chadbourne suggests that the essay "is both fragmentary and complete in itself, capable both of standing on its own and of forming a kind of 'higher organism' when assembled with other essays by its author." *Hidden Cargoes* is precisely such a beast. All of its constituent body parts contribute to what the "higher organism" is concerned with— namely, exploring the extraordinary nature of the ordinary.

A Kist o' Whistles

It weighs almost nothing when I place it on my palm. Left there, it would soon become blood-warmed, almost to the temperature it had when it was alive. I'm holding an owl's skull. Or, to be more exact, I'm holding the skull of a long-eared owl (*Asio otus*). The bird it was part of died fifty years ago, caught in a cull of crows in a small wood in Northern Ireland. The perpetrators fired indiscriminately into the trees after dark, when the crows were roosting. I found the owl's body lying among the intended victims—the ground littered with telltale shotgun shells, their orange cases peppering with garish, unnatural color the dull scatter of feathered bodies lying among the leaves. I lifted the owl gently, cradling its limpness, and took it home.

I kept two of the primary wing feathers, their surface furred with velvety down, their leading edges delicately serrated, like fine-toothed combs. These adaptations channel and hush the passage of the air and allow the owl to fly with deadly silence, giving its prey no warning of a predator's approach. Having put the feathers aside, I sheathed the owl's corpse in a sarcophagus of wire netting and buried it in the garden. I marked the spot with a piece of slate, pushed into the ground like a miniature headstone, the date of burial scratched across it. After ten weeks I dug it up. The detritivores had done their work, little grave robbers of the flesh. Only the skeleton was left, safely immovable within its cage. I cleaned the skull with diluted bleach, rinsed it, then left it in the sun to dry and whiten. I've kept it ever since.

I realize this may seem macabre. Isn't a sloughed-off body part a distasteful—even repulsive—souvenir? Those who see it thus would shy away from touching it. If their fingers brushed against it accidentally, it might spark enough disgust to make them want to scrub their hands, or even shower, rid themselves of a sense of dirt, pollution, death. To me, it is a treasured token of a time and place I remember with great fondness. Far from being revolted by its corporeality, I marvel at the skull's fragile beauty, at what it once contained, at what it *is*.

I like to weigh it in my hand, rekindle in my imagination the story that's invisibly imbued in it. Once, this husk-like remnant was the fortress behind whose walls a brain lay, protected, pulsing with the energy that vivified it. This was the bony cockpit from which a flood of sensations was savored and controlled as life's currents thrummed through the assembled cells, their pulse and voltage aligned in precisely the patterns needed to fit the niche of existence the bird occupied, carved out with exquisite particularity over the millennia. Although this relic is so light it feels like almost nothing, it carries a heavy cargo. I hope the reliquary of words I'm making for it here can contain and convey the electricity of wonder that I still feel crackling around it.

Thornybrook Wood, County Antrim.

I've changed the name, of course, disguised the location, wary of leaving a trail for egg collectors — or the merely careless curious. Once comparatively wild and rarely visited, as the Belfast-Lisburn conurbation continued its advance, engulfing countryside with a spread of roads and houses, the proximity and density of people increased. Soon it came to constitute a threat. Places like Thornybrook Wood are vulnerable. When I went there as a teenager it was rare to encounter anybody else — except an occasional, solitary angler fishing for brown trout in the nearby lake. Part of what made the shooting of the owl so shocking was its testimony of human incursion into this unfrequented place. The litter of spent ammunition was unwelcome evidence of other people's presence in what I considered, I know unreasonably, to be my wood.

This was somewhere I got to know with the intimacy of spending unhurried hours there, just being in the place, listening to its sounds, attentive to its sights and smells, savoring its tastes, feeling the sun upon my skin, and the smooth, warm suck and tug of mud as I waded through the marshy ground around the lake, searching for orchids, or to reach a moorhen's nest. I can remember, as if yesterday, the wind shushing through the bulrushes, rippling the water with its breath. I remember, too, the sense of expectant wariness I felt the moment I stepped into the wood itself, knowing that the trees enclosed a little kingdom set apart from the adjoining fields and populated with its own watchful denizens.

It took an hour to cycle to Thornybrook from

where we lived. In those days, traffic was infrequent. I'd see a dozen vehicles at most once I'd left the town. The wood covered an area of several acres, cladding with its mix of deciduous trees and conifers a small rise of land that was bordered on one side by a lake and on the other by a river and marshy fields. Standing at the edge of the wood and looking across the rural panorama stretching toward the distant summits of the hills above Belfast, there were only a few scattered farmhouses; most of the outlook was the green of fields and trees and hedges. The area was rich in plant and animal life. It had a profusion of wildflowers, many species of bird; hares were a frequent sight. There was always evidence of foxes and badgers in the wood; and hedgehogs, weasels, stoats, and otters were often glimpsed. Summer brought an abundance of insects. The dragonflies were particularly striking, and I saw butterflies and moths there that I've not seen anywhere else. For me, it was a special place.

In fact, when I think about it now, I'm tempted to delete *special* and write *magical,* or even *sacred.* Thornybrook generated a sense of being part of a fabric of life that was woven with a richer, brighter mix of thread than anything the town could offer. I felt more alive there. Though I know it had no grandeur, wasn't anywhere of note, possessed no special features that would warrant mention in a tourist guidebook, to me these rough acres of the County Antrim countryside possessed a rare beauty that touched me far more deeply than any of the world's famous picturesque places. The reputation of such places drew me to visit in the years ahead, but they always left me feeling disap-

pointed, curiously empty, let down by the somehow run-of-the-mill splendor of their vaunted sce-
nic-ness.

I'm not sure if I can explain Thornybrook's
impact on me; it's something I don't fully understand myself. But a key factor was surely that my
own psychophysical season made me suscepti-
ble to what I think of as the spirit of this place.
It felt like the isobars that controlled my inner
climate swirled their way outwards and became
comfortably entangled with Thornybrook's, inner
and outer weathers falling snugly into step. I ex-
plored the area in my early teens, when the fluc-
tuating energies of adolescence were at their peak.
Enthusiasms, interests, passionate attachments
and dislikes surged through me with disorientat-
ing strength. Being in the wood I felt anchored,
grounded, as if this was somewhere the voltage
of my youth could safely earth. And, as it did, a
reciprocal but calming current seemed to flow into
me from the place itself. There was a strong sense
of connection, even entanglement—of land an-
swering flesh, water and blood singing together,
pulse beating synchronously with pulse.

I hope this image of reciprocity at least hints at
what I felt. It was as if I became benignly sutured
to the place, my sense of self running its tendrils
on into the trees and field and hedges, and they in
turn giving something of their nature back to me.
Watching sticklebacks and minnows in the sun-
warmed lakeside shallows; climbing a spruce tree
to find a sparrowhawk's nest; watching a heron
hunting frogs; listening to a cuckoo calling; being
startled by a snipe taking off at my feet; encountering a family of foxes at dusk; hearing bats and

seeing their shapes flitting wraithlike through the dark; and, yes, lifting a dead owl from amidst the crows and leaves and cartridge cases—these and countless other interactions with what happened there kindled a sense of communion, of something flowing from the land to me and back again. One of the reasons the owl's skull has become such a potent talisman is that it's a token of this sense of intimate melding—an unlicensed, outlaw Eucharist.

Though the skull is empty now, the shape of this fantastical container holds in its curves and hollows sufficient prompts to nudge into mind a picture of what once was here, held securely in its place, cradled in this little crucible. Sometimes I think of it as a kind of haunted house, its tiny chambers still ghosted with the presences that used to occupy it. Chief among them are the eyes—possessing, in life, striking orange-yellow coronas rimming the black irises. All that remains to suggest them now are the two massive hollows on either side of the skull. These, and the large ear cavities behind them, are testimony to the exquisitely acute sensory array brought to bear in hunting. The long-eared owl, as John Burton notes in *Owls of the World: Their Evolution, Structure and Ecology*, "is one of the most nocturnal owls in the world." Accordingly, their eyes are designed to operate in near total darkness, their ears calibrated to detect with pinpoint accuracy the rustle of tiny movements in the dark. The left ear opening is set slightly higher in the skull than the right one, an asymmetry that further enhances the bird's skill in

directional location. Sounds reach one ear fractionally sooner than the other, and the time difference
provides a kind of aural pincer of extraordinary fi-
nesse. It lets the owl locate where a noise has come
from with millimetric precision. In *The Secret Life
of the Owl*, John Lewis-Stempel estimates that their
hearing is honed to such a pitch that "owls are capable of detecting time differences of as little as 30
millionths of a second."

Looking at the skull, I'm struck by the fact that
it's the apportioning of spaces, the relative size of
the emptinesses it encloses, that's as suggestive of
the bird's nature as any solid structure—though
the hooked beak, still with a cuticle of dark, horny
matter sheathing the white bone, clearly announc-
es predatory function in its shape and sharpness.
Behind the eye sockets and the cavities for the ears,
the quayside to which these organs were once anchored, there's the gently domed occipital bone,
the housing for the brain. There are openings between it and the eyes and ears, the bone plating
of the braincase pierced with apertures, showing
where dense cablings of nerves used to run. At the
skull's base is the largest aperture of all—the fora-
men magnum—the carriageway connecting brain
to spinal cord.

After diverging from their common reptilian
ancestor millions of years ago, mammalian and
avian brains followed slightly different structur-
al routes. In mammals, intelligence resides mainly in the cortex. In birds, it's sited in what Frank
Gill, in his magisterial textbook *Ornithology*, calls
"an alternative and unique feature," namely, "the
hyperstriatum and associated Wulst." I put my
finger to where that would have been, the spark

of intelligence burning just behind the delicately crafted bulges of the bone, hard beneath my touch, but wafer thin—an almost translucent chrysalis.

The visual and auditory spaces outlined by the bony tracery of the skull—the enormous empty sockets and behind them the asymmetrical coves for listening—beckon back eyes and ears. Prompted by these cephalic cues, and by what I remember from watching living owls, it's not hard to picture the skull filled with a brain again, enfleshed and feathered, part of a breathing, moving bird. It stretches out its wings, looks at me with its strange, yellow-circled eyes, and flies silently away, to hunt in my store of memories.

The owls were a key ingredient in the enchantment I felt Thornybook Wood possessed. Knowing that it was home to these rarely seen nocturnal creatures enhanced the spell the place exerted. The fact that the rhythm of their existence was played out here, a long-established presence, bestowed a kind of secret pulse. In taking it—by occasional sightings, by finding a dropped feather, by collecting owl pellets—I felt attuned to the music of the place. The owls played a cadenza that you had to listen hard for, but once your ear became attuned and you learned to recognize its notes, they exerted a siren allure. The virtuosity of their lives is breathtaking.

I spent hours at dusk and nightfall crouching motionless, concealed in the hawthorn hedge that edged a field facing that part of the wood the owls favored for their daytime roost. To see their large, silent shapes take form as they slid from the trees and flew low and silent across the grass was something I found thrilling each time I witnessed it. Once, one flew straight towards me, level with my face. It banked and curved at what seemed like the last moment, only seconds from collision. When I whipped round, I was in time to see it disappearing across the next field that stretched out behind my hiding place.

In daylight I searched for pellets—owls swallow their prey whole and later cough up what's indigestible in pellets containing fur, feather, bone, and the shiny chitin of beetles' wing cases. Sometimes I found fresh pellets clumped telltale under a roost so that, looking up, I was able to make out the pale shape of an owl sitting quite still above me in a tree, its body pressed close against the trunk. Once the eye learns to pick it out, to read color instead of camouflage, the plumage is beautiful, an intricate mix of subtle patterns, interweaving browns and creams and buffs. I've climbed to nests—untidy affairs without evidence of crafting, little more than rough, twiggy platforms provided by the old nests of other birds. I've seen eggs—white orbs, improbably pure and perfect in their ramshackle surroundings, gravid with the promise of new life. And I've exchanged looks with owlets, blinking like tiny aliens as they sit, still flightless, in the high branches beside the nest, improbably strange-looking creatures, covered in down, the huge eyes and tufts of feathers starting to show through, making them seem both weird and comic. I've dissected pellets and worked out the owl's diet from the remnants left in these tiny ossuaries, laying out their load of bones and identifying them by matching them against remains held in labelled museum collections. But by far my most striking memories of Thornybrook are of seeing the owls hunting, watching their ghostly forms materializing like a kind of solid darkness in the half-light of dusk. In those days, in that place, I was attuned to owls, which meant I was greatly saddened by the waste of losing one so casually, so pointlessly, in the ill-considered slaughter of another species.

It's impossible to be sure if the skull belonged to one of the owls I saw hunting. Over the time I spent at Thornybrook, I had many owl sightings. It's hard to tell how many different birds that involved and if this skull was once part of one of them. One long-eared owl looks just like another; there are no obvious differences between the sexes, though the females are slightly larger than the males. Usually my sightings were only momentary and often in poor light, so that even if there had been slight individual variations in different birds, they'd have been effectively invisible. Most years I found a single nest (others may have eluded my search). One season I found two, but that doesn't necessarily mean much in itself; a pair may move from one nest site to another. Though John Sparks and Tony Soper, in *Owls: Their Natural and Unnatural History*, say that long-eared owls sometimes "form communal roosts," I've never seen more than two adult birds together at the same time, though I did once see four juveniles. I don't know how long the fledged young stay in the vicinity. Nor do I know how often nonresident owls passed through the wood, looking for food or mates, or perhaps just blown off course in difficult weather. I don't know what the typical hunting range of a long-eared owl is. Perhaps Thornybrook was regularly visited by fly-ins from elsewhere. It could have been one of those that had the ill luck to be caught in the nighttime massacre.

Despite these uncertainties, I think the strong likelihood is that the owl I found dead among the crows was one of those I'd seen alive. So when I balance the skull on my palm, examine its structure, muse about its story, I often wonder if I featured in it. Did I play a bit part in its drama? Did this now-fragile receptacle once hold within the maze of its living brain an image of my teenage self? Did the ears pick up my footsteps, the eyes take in my shape? I find it curiously pleasing to think that here, within this bony chamber, an awareness of my presence may once have flickered across the bird's notice, something of me translated into nerve impulses speeding through the brain. It's intriguing to speculate about how I'd register on an owl's sensorium. I don't know how a human shape or human noises — breathing, footsteps, cough and rustle, laugh and voice — would be read by this secretive nocturnal predator. How I would have appeared to it would almost certainly not be in any form I'd recognize as me.

Much of the skull's magnetism, what charges it with the significance it has, stems from my sense of it as a token taken from somewhere that was pivotal in my growing up. Somehow it still seems imbued with the flavour of the time I spent there. I know there's nothing left in it; its emptiness is quite complete. This flimsy relic enfolds within its fragile walls only the nothingness of vanished tenure. Yet for me it carries a precious, invisible cargo. When I hold it, it's as if its vanished eyes and ears pour back into my grip a distillation of the sights and sounds they gathered as they scanned the contours around Thornybrook. The skull provides a kind of spyhole, a magic lens that lets me see across time and space to zero in on Thornybrook Wood as it existed, unspoiled, half a century ago, and on me as the youth I used to be, just emerging into adulthood.

I sometimes think of the owl's skull as a kind of space probe, launched into the little planetary system of Thornybrook Wood and its environs. For the duration of the owl's life, obedient as any satellite, it gathered data from this place, sifting through the signals that its senses harvested as they netted what pulsed out from the fields, the trees, the lake, and the bodies of prey creatures. Reading the input that it garnered, the owl settled into its daily — nightly — orbits, held in the cradle of life offered here, in this place, at that time, in a particular manner — the niche that sustained it. The ill-chance of its death, being caught in the cull of crows, again points to its perfectly crafted adaptations for nocturnal hunting. As that doyen of ornithological photographers Eric Hosking puts it, in his autobiography *An Eye for a Bird,* "in the dark this owl is able to fly safely through dense forests, with intertwining branches." Had it not been flying through the trees when the cullers were firing into the branches, the only bodies left for me to find would have been crows.

Though the individual owl concerned perished

half a century ago, this skull its only remnant, I
hope that other owls, perhaps the descendants of
this one, still occupy that niche. I know a lot has
changed at Thornybrook, that human encroach-
ment has massively increased, but I hope — perhaps unrealistically — that enough remains to provide a refuge for these beautiful birds. If they've
gone, it would be another sad impoverishment
of place. To grasp what their loss entails, think of
what these birds represent beyond the individual feathered forms we see roosting in a tree or
flying through the night. Every individual looks
back to the breeding pair before it. Each bird I saw
at Thornybrook is the present point on a bloodline that stretches back for millions of years. The
"oldest known record of an owl," says John Lewis-Stempel, "is from about 58 million years ago."
Through that stupendous span of time, impulses
have travelled along owl nerves, receptors of a
barrage of information from the world's different
habitats. Those impulses have been sifted, honed,
and organized to create the diverse patterns of life
of the many owl species that developed, *Asio otus*
among them. Think of the accumulated messages
passing from owl eyes and owl ears to owl brains,
think of the impulses coursing through the inner
kingdom of the owl, commanding talon clutch-
es, beak yawns, wing stretches, glides, pounces
on prey, and coughing-up of pellets. Think of the
time taken to issue in these different forms of life,
to carve out their patterns, to exactly fit their niches. Then think of it snuffed out. Each individual
bird is astonishing enough in its own right, in its
single life. Seen as a fingerprint upon the Earth
of the history of its kind, it's so extraordinary it

appears miraculous.

I know that if I closed my hand and squeezed, even gently, the skull would shatter. The living bone would have possessed robust tensile strength. But severed from life's throb and fizz it's become a brittle husk. It has about it now an air of eggshell fragility. Sometimes I think it would be best to take it back to Thornybrook, pulverize it in my hand, and let the wind blow the dust and fragments back into the embrace of the place that once sustained it. But I value it too much to give it back. Nor do I wish to revisit Thornybrook; I have no wish to see a place I loved as what I fear it may be now. Judging by what I saw the last time I was in Ireland, it's well on its way to being denuded of its specialness. It was littered and besmirched by overuse. I saw evidence of careless tree felling, hedges ripped up, fields made into building sites, and everywhere you looked there were clusters of new houses. The land was thread-veined with roads not there before, riven with traffic noise, the wood become a haunt of too many dog walkers.

So the skull sits on my bookshelf, acting like a tiny beacon that marks the features of a now almost-mythical-seeming coastline. It pulses out a signal of a kind of phantom geography, hinting at the contours of another time and place, and a way of being that's under threat, or maybe vanished already. Despite its dryness, it acts like a kind of reservoir, holding accumulated sensations and flooding the imagination with memories, remembered panoramas, images, ideas. As well as registering some picture of my teenage self, did the skull once hold the clatter and din of the army helicopters that often flew low over the wood? How did such a monstrous, alien noise impinge on hearing sensitive enough to catch the rustle of a pygmy-shrew and pinpoint precisely where the movement came from? Did the owl's night vision glimpse the furtive figures of terrorists hiding arms at the abandoned farmhouse, later raided by police, or see them lying in wait to spring an ambush? Northern Ireland's Troubles were raging at that time. They foisted on remote, unfrequented places like Thornybrook a dark tenancy as secretive as that of owls, but far from welcome.

The owl's skull often nudges into mind a picture of the moment that the bird was killed. The sound of gunfire would have carried across the lake, a loud intrusion in the quiet of a peaceful place. If I'd been in the wood that night, would I have heard the rain-like pitter of lead shot ripping through the leaves, or would that deadly sound have been masked, overlaid with the cullers' shouts and the loud detonations of their shots as they fired into the trees? Would I have heard the repeated thump of feathered bodies as they hit the ground, like giant cushioned hailstones? What was the last sensation that registered in the owl's brain, encoded in the network of nerve impulses that flickered through the warm tissue that once filled this skull? The noise, the shapes of people, the impact when it fell? A sense—however such a sense might be mapped and parsed within an owl's cognition—of bewilderment, disorientation, terror? Trying to picture the last spark of awareness that shimmered through this bony container in my hand makes me think about the first moment of consciousness hosted within it. Would it have been a sense of swaying and warmth, as the embryo neared hatching in the egg, the nest rocked gently in a windblown tree, the adult bird's body generating an incubating heat? Between these two points, first and last sensations, the beginning and end of life, what symphony of sights and sounds played through the skull's now-emptied concert hall? And echoing this question on a species scale, what were the first sensations that could be attributed to *Asio otus*? What will be the final ones in the last surviving members of this bloodline? And what, cumulatively, does the music of their saga sound like? What does it all amount to?

The metaphor of music calls to mind a Scottish expression, "kist o' whistles." It means a church organ. A kist is simply a chest or large box. Originally, *kist o' whistles* had a derogatory, mocking ring to it. But as the term passed out of common parlance and into literary use, that negative slant evaporated. I first heard it years ago, when I fled Northern Ireland's violence to live in Scotland. *Kist o' whistles* made an instant appeal. I just liked the sound of it. It's not something I would have thought of using until now. For me, it was more an etymological curio than part of my working vocabulary, a quaint-sounding term rather than a useful one. But it surely fits the owl's skull beautifully. For is it not a treasure chest of whistles? The intimate array of microtubing that once filled it—threading the brain's tissue with veins, arteries, capillaries, nerves—is like a complex array of living organ pipes. I warm to the idea of the skull as a bony musical box sounding out the intricate toccatas and fugues of owl life. The way *kist* is used as a verb adds to the sense of fit. To kist a body, or kisting a body, is to coffin it, so a *kist o' whistles* not only catches the sense of the owl's music and the skull's boxlike containment of it, it also taps into the funereal thread of the story, the sombre note of death. And the connotations with church and sacred music are also ironically apt— because I always found Thornybrook and its owls had far more sense of numen than I ever felt sitting in a hard-backed pew, surrounded by the niceties of conventional faith.

The other association that surprised me when I began to write about the skull, coming back to mind as unbidden as a *kist o' whistles,* is something from a fifteenth-century medical treatise, the *Hortus Sanitatis*. The title means "Garden of Health, "and the book is a compendium of supposed cures. It provides a wealth of information, much of it dubious, about the medicinal use of plants and animals. It includes remedies based on the body parts of a whole range of creatures, both real and imaginary. One cure for insanity suggests placing an owl's ashes on the eyes of the person afflicted. Perhaps if the reliquary I've written here has any use, it lies in the hope that the words it contains might act like ash, fall on afflicted eyes, cure them of the lack of vision that has allowed us to sleepwalk our way to the loss of so many Thornybrooks.

Ear Piece

Enshrining the Hair of Strangers (i)

Two hairs have fallen on my leg.
They're not mine.
One is Australian, the other Scottish.
The Australian hair is long, black, straight.
The Scottish one is grey and frizzy.
Without thinking I brush them off.
Now, I wish I hadn't.

They offered tokens of remembrance from the unexpected pilgrimage I was drawn into. But who keeps the hairs of strangers? To preserve them would be verging on the ghoulish. Their retention, far from providing talismans of the moment, would suggest a distasteful readiness to collect things too intimately connected with other people's bodies to turn into souvenirs.

The hairs having gone and, in any case, the keeping of them being suspect, I'll content myself with enshrining them in this word-picture.

That the grey hair had fallen was no surprise. In fact, it seems odd that there weren't more. The woman's hair cascaded untidily over her head and shoulders. Swarmed with an occupying army of grey, this once-brown mane still possessed a wild exuberance. That it might colonize territory beyond the space its bearer occupied seemed in keeping with its hard-to-contain character. I could picture the woman shedding it thickly in her wake, a profligate seeding that yet wouldn't cause any noticeable diminution in its abundance.

But the black hair was another matter.

I'd not have expected any strands of it to escape the marshalling that kept them all so neatly in place.

The two hairs set the scene by reminding me that if the girl's hair had been allowed to fall loose, been given the freedom of her grey-haired companion's, what lay beneath it wouldn't have been revealed and I'd never have been drawn into the labyrinth that it contained.

Ear (i)

Her long black hair is tied back and braided so that her ears are left completely exposed. Each time she turns to speak to the grey-haired woman sitting beside her, her left ear is placed directly in my line of sight.
It's hard not to look at it.
Its naked whorls beckon my eye.

I try not to stare, try not to be intrusive; I know I should adopt the detachment that's expected. The unspoken etiquette of public transport demands that we don't subject each other to intense scrutiny; a casual, passing glance is all that's allowed. But the girl's ear is only fifteen inches from my eye. If I blew gently, she'd feel my breath on it. Her ear tugs at my attention as surely as a whirlpool sucks small craft to its center. I can't stop myself from stealing more than the single sanctioned glance that's scarcely taken before you're meant to look away.

My Brother's Voice (i)

I'm lost.
Give me some bearings.

Where are we?
Who are these people?
What kind of pilgrimage are you making?

I need coordinates of time and place. You have to set the scene. Readers will want names and descriptions. They need an idea of what people look like, where they're going, and why they're in such close proximity to you that their hairs are falling in your lap.

That's his response to a first draft of this piece — we often swap what we're writing for sibling comment. My brother is impatient for the kind of detail that in truth doesn't much interest me. But I guess fallen hairs, talk of going on an unexpected pilgrimage, and becoming fixated by a girl's ear might need some linking context, otherwise presenting them together may seem little more than a random assemblage of unrelated items.

So, briefly, here's the background.

Perth Bus Station, Scotland

They're in the seat in front of me.

The driver hasn't started the engine yet so there's no muting thrum of background noise to mask their words. I can't help overhearing their conversation. Although the bus is full, no one else in my immediate vicinity is talking so everything they say is clearly audible. They're not talking about anything private. But I still feel uncomfortable as an eavesdropper, however unchosen a role it is.

The Australian girl is in her twenties. She's suntanned, black haired, slimly shapely. She exudes a youthful vigor that suggests robust raw health. The perfume that plays about her contains an unmistakable element of patchouli. By contrast, the woman beside her is in her forties, overweight, with a pasty indoor pallor. She has the look of someone who's experienced hardship but whose reserves of strength haven't been exhausted by it. Her mass of untidy hair alone suggests energy to spare. Judging by the smell that clings to her — now tinged with patchouli — she's a heavy smoker. The two of them seem relaxed in themselves and easy in each other's company. Both display a ready friendliness and warmth. When the Australian girl sat down in the seat next to her, the older woman turned and smiled. Soon they were chatting. The alternation of Scottish and Australian accents brings an exotic music to the banalities they exchange.

At first they talk about how unseasonably cold it is for springtime, and how crowded the bus is for a late-morning service. But soon they move on to exchange information about themselves. I discover that the Australian girl is from "the other Perth," as she puts it. She's in Perth, Scotland, to trace her ancestry. Her great great-grandmother was born in nearby Scone. She was there earlier this morning searching for a headstone in the cemetery. The woman with the unruly hair is Perth born and bred. One of her sons visited Australia a few years ago and loved it. She has a cousin who lives in Scone. The bus we're all on is for Dundee. The Australian girl is going there on her way to St. Andrews, where she's enrolled as a student for a year, part of an exchange scheme with her university at home. The woman from Perth is going to visit her daughter — and first grandchild — in Dundee.

I'm sorry, Brother, I don't know their names. Nor do I think it's necessary to describe them in more detail. (Does it matter what they're wear-ing?) And I don't feel much inclined to paint a ver-bal picture of Perth bus station, or of my fellow passengers; neither are particularly noteworthy.

The bus starts and the vibrations of the engine, plus the traffic noise outside, coupled with the ambient sounds of maybe thirty people shifting in their seats, coughing, talking on their phones, rus-tling newspapers, etc., means that I can no longer make out what the Australian girl and the woman from Perth are saying. They continue chatting all the way to Dundee, but I'm no longer forced to overhear.

The Australian girl's left ear continues to captivate me.

Each time she turns to her companion, it's exposed closely to my view.

Ear (ii)

What's more ordinary than an ear?

And yet what's utterly astonishing sits there with it, hidden — not hidden — in plain sight.

Unusually for someone of her generation, the girl's ear is unpierced, unadorned. Its cupped swirls and ridges, the softly budded swell in the dangle of the lobe, the skin's tone and tautness, the faint covering of down that furs the surface — ev-erything about it blooms with youth. It glows with aliveness, is gravid with the beauty of corporeal perfection. Exposed by her tied-back, braided hair, the ear's complete nakedness imbues it with a vul-nerability, a secrecy, a sense of something intimate and innocent uncovered.

To look feels like trespass.

Not to look requires more restraint than I can

summon.

Shells are a common comparison used in descriptions of the ear. Indeed whispering in someone's "shell-like" is a common colloquialism. But however similar to a shell in its sculpting an ear may be, I think this metaphor is a poor one — both because of the dissimilarity in texture and temperature, and because a shell encloses, protects, hides, while an ear beckons and invites, funneling a myriad of sounds into the brain's eager receptivity. One keeps the world out; the other draws it in. Maybe the comparison gained some credence from the way we used to put the pink-lipped mouths of empty conch shells to our ears when we were children. It's said that when you do this you can hear the sea. Of course what's heard is simply the secret tide of the body's own interiority washing and whispering its waves within us. Hearing it, as we held the conch's little echo chamber tightly pressed against our heads, perhaps made the shell-ear link seem plausible.

I'm not much taken with the comparison to a shell, but I warm to the idea of an oceanic dimension to the ear.

Looking — not looking — at the Australian girl's ear, thinking of all the sounds that will pour into it over her lifetime, I get a definite sense of something pelagic in terms of flow and surge and scale.

Even now, in the modest span of years it has existed, it will have taken in an enormous aural tide:

voices
birdsong
doors opening and closing
car engines revving

wind rushing through trees
dentists' drills
singing
crying
fireworks
raindrops' staccato against windows
aircraft overhead
playground noises
music
dogs panting, barking
gunfire
hot fat sizzling in a frying pan
the roar of surf on one of the other Perth's
    beaches

I picture her as an infant taking her first un-steady steps along Cottesloe's warm sand, hands held by her parents, a reassuring presence on each side, their voices already laying down a bedrock of familiarity in the slowly filling reservoir of her hearing, touchstones whose repeated utterance will provide love's safe anchorage and her sense of home.

To write a cargo manifest of sounds heard over her lifetime would quickly become unman-ageable; such an itemization would effectively be endless.

My Brother's Voice (ii)

Okay, I get it that you stared at a pretty girl's ear to pass the time on your bus journey. I'd still like a name for her, though, and to know more about her story. Why not call her Jilly or Leah and provide some background? Is the bus travelling through a featureless white void? You need to describe the countryside you're passing through. Even if you don't want to describe the other passengers, can't you at least tell us something about the driver? And I still don't get it about the pilgrimage. What do you mean by that?

Though I like to bounce my writing off him, the problem with my brother is that he prefers things cut and dried. He reads a lot but abandons books in disgust if he can't get a handle on things early on, picture the main characters in his mind's eye, or follow a story's progression from a beginning through a middle to an end. He doesn't like it if anything is left unresolved, or if a writer embarks on a digression. Novels that finish "up in the air" he finds particularly irksome; loose ends annoy him. He's got a good eye for typographical error and slips in grammar, but he likes everything too neatly tied up for my taste.

Life's an untidy business, I remind him, and this is life-writing, so I can't just invent things or smooth them over with a made-up story line.

But he wants nonfiction to give him what he calls "the whole picture" rather than teasing fragments, and it should proceed, he says, in an ordered, logical fashion.

I sigh.

There's an inevitable fragmentariness about what I can observe, and it lacks any neat, point-by-point unfolding.

I don't know names.

Most of the background is hidden from me.

The idea of presenting the whole picture is ridiculous! Our experience is inevitably partial, rarely logical, mostly unstructured.

In any case, it's not plain observation and documentary that interest me; it's the ideas sparked by what I see.

As for the countryside outside the window, it doesn't matter. Whether we're crossing a river, driving past fields, or going through a town, the passing landscape won't affect the way the girl's ear strikes me. It would make no difference if we were travelling between two suburbs of Australian Perth on a Transdev bus rather than between Scottish Perth and Dundee on this Stagecoach service.

You wanted to know about the driver. Well, he has a tattoo of the dancing Shiva on his left forearm. I noticed it when I was buying my ticket. But I don't know if being marked with this Hindu symbol means he has sympathies for, or belongs to, that religion, or if he got it as a souvenir from holidaying in India. Maybe he just likes the design. I don't know how much, if at all, he understands the symbolism of this ancient diagram of existence. In short, I'm not sure how to read his dancing Shiva tattoo.

Our experience of the world is full of such shards of people's stories — splinters that catch the eye but whose history you'll never discover, whose significance you can only guess at.

As for *pilgrimage*, yes, I'll concede that — initially (but only initially) — this may sound like the wrong word.

It's not as if I made a trek to some sacred site; I endured no physical hardships along the way. I had no prayer beads, no holy books about my person. I didn't fast or meditate, didn't prepare myself spiritually, or undergo purification rituals before stepping on the bus. I didn't shave my head or don special robes. It's not as if I'm a religious person.

Despite this, the thought-journey the girl's ear prompted seemed closer to something sacred than to the everyday secularities that characterize a commonplace bus journey. If an ear takes on an almost numinous quality, Brother, if it leads me into a maze of ideas and associations that are frankly amazing — and humbling — is my encounter with them not more akin to pilgrimage than to my ordinary pedestrian progress through a day?

Ear (iii)

What were the first sounds to cross the threshold of her infant auricle and travel down her virginal ear canal, penetrating deep into the soft, convoluted recesses of her newborn brain?

Whose was the first voice she was aware of?

What were the first words she understood, the alchemy of hearing issuing in the gold of sense?

Whose voice will be the last one she ever hears and what will it say to her before her hearing flickers out for good?

Will she hear truth spoken more than lies?

Will she take delight in recognizing the lilting song of goldfinches, or will she be deaf to such small-scale sublimities of natural sound?

How often will "I love you" be whispered to her? How often meant?

What spoken syllables will bring her greatest pleasure?

What words will break her heart?

I try to picture the intricate processes involved as the world's noises repeatedly nudge her awareness: how the auditory ossicles, the trinity of hammer-anvil-stirrup — the body's tiniest bones — catch vibrations from the eardrum and pass them to the cochlea, whose little reservoir of liquid is stirred into waves, their waters fished by scores of tiny hairs whose catch creates the nerve signals that the brain can read. But the delicacy, speed, and complexity of what happens makes any images I cast in words seem lumbering by comparison.

Looked at in one way, the Australian girl's ear speaks of her individuality. It's like her fingerprints or signature. The precise lineaments of its curvature and sculpting, the angle at which it's affixed to her skull, its temperature and hue, its odor, texture, thickness, and the enormous catalogue of what it's heard — these are all highly specific, part of the fine detail of who she is, features that help define the unique particularity of her one, never-to-be-repeated life story.

But *look at it another way,* and her ear echoes millions like it. Its uniqueness disappears, and its common coin of design and purpose buys into far wider perspectives.

Word-minting (i)

"Look at it another way . . ."

That looking — and the wider perspectives it opens up — requires a different word.

Looking by itself is not enough.

Looking suggests a focus that's simply on the girl's ear as it exists right now in front of me. But I'm not just looking in this straightforward sense of examining an ear that's fifteen inches away from me. Doing so prompts another sort of vision, switches the mind into an entirely different gear. There's no word for it, but there should be so I'll make one: *timescan.* Here's how I define it.

> *Timescan* (verb): To look at something not just as it appears at the present

moment, but rather as it is over the full span of time that it occupies or suggests. For example, if a person was timescanned, they'd appear not as the person you see in front of you but as a changing entity that starts as a fertilized egg, develops into an embryo, baby, infant, child, young person, adult, old person, and corpse. Radical timescanning goes further—looking beyond the individual to the bloodline of ancestors without whose meeting and mating the individual in question wouldn't exist. The bloodline of descendants who point into the future may also be taken into account. Timescanning is a mode of seeing that relies partly on the eyes, mainly on the imagination.

I'm timescanning the Australian girl's ear, not just looking at it. This means I see it not just in terms of the minutes it occupies as we're sitting on a bus between Perth and Dundee, but in terms of the temporal horizons that come into view when its wider nature is considered, horizons that stretch out for eons beyond these brief moments of encounter.

Ear (iv)

It's easy to think that the full time-span of the girl's ear runs between two clearly marked points: the moment when the embryo she started out as first developed recognizable ears, and the likely conclusion of her story, the moment when the old woman she'll become is pronounced dead and her ears grow cold as the body heat leaves her cadaver.

But this Australian girl's ear, like any ear, is part of a far more ancient lineage than such a simply drawn individual lifeline suggests. The point of genesis isn't the moment of her conception—that's just a staging post along the way. To radically timescan her ear is to see it as something pointing back to the chain of ancestors that led to her—parents, grandparents, great-grandparents—that Scone great-grandmother and all the increasingly shadowy forbears stretching back and back before her. They lead eventually from history into prehistory, and from our cave-dwelling days into the stratum of deep time and prehuman forms in which our origins lie hidden. And if she has children, who in turn have children of their own, the story of her ear continues, perhaps as far into the future as it does into the past. Her ear is part of a timeline that's of almost inconceivable duration. Its richly diverse, changing nature is difficult to fathom. I picture it as a long, snaking filament smudged with the multiple sound prints that have laid their touch on human (and prehuman) hearing—the cries of long-extinct animals, the words of languages no longer spoken, the roar of ancient seas, the voices of countless vanished individuals.

The Australian girl's ear is the tip of an iceberg-archive that's bathed in the supersaturate of sounds that have happened in our passage through the ages.

All this is implicit in the ear that's so close I could reach out and touch it. Yes, I know, it's just an ear—one of billions in the world—but it also acts like a secret portal that gives access to the labyrinth of being. It beckons me deep into time's conduits. They lead to territory so far removed from the familiar moments of a bus journey that it's hard to credit there's a connection between them.

Dundee Bus Station, Scotland

We arrive in Dundee and everyone gets off the bus. The dark-haired Australian girl and the grey-haired Scottish woman stop amidst the throng of people milling around the bus station. They hug each other, exchange smiles, then go their separate ways, turning once, as if somehow synchronized, to wave. The girl gets on a 99C bus for St Andrews that's already waiting, engine running, at Stance 4; the woman exits towards the city center. I join the queue for a bus to Aberdeen. As I'm waiting, the 99C reverses and then drives away. The Australian girl is sitting next to a window, her left ear clearly visible.

I almost feel like waving to it as I watch the bus drive out of sight.

My Brother's Voice (iii)

Is that it? I mean, for an ending?

You're standing in a bus queue and "almost feel like waving" to a girl's ear. A girl's ear, I mean, really? You've not spoken to her. You don't know who she is. Beyond your minimal description — suntanned, black haired, slimly shapely — we don't know what she looks like; I can only form the vaguest of images. She disappears from the scene on the 99C bus and that's all there is. We don't know what happens to her, whether she and the frizzy-haired woman will ever meet again. Surely some resolution is needed, some kind of conclusion. Without it, readers are bound to feel puzzled and let down. It would be like abandoning a piece mid-

sentence to end it here; it's horribly anticlimactic. You need to craft a proper sense of an ending, not just stop with a vague inclination to wave at someone's ear, an inclination you didn't even act on.

I find it frustrating too, Brother. But endings are just literary inventions; life goes on in its complicated, messy fashion. I can imagine all sorts of more satisfying ways things might have turned out. The corny old romantic in me even toys with a hackneyed scenario that would have me and the Australian girl exchanging names, talking, walking off arm in arm into the proverbial sunset to live (of course) happily ever after. It's curious that such a fatuous conclusion would satisfy you in a way reality doesn't.

All that happened can be summed up in a few words: "I thought about the ear of the girl who was sitting in front of me on the bus from Perth to Dundee. Then I went my way and she went hers. Our paths won't cross again. I've no idea who she is, or how things will play out in her life. She didn't even notice me. If she knew about my timescanning of her ear, I don't know what she'd make of it."

That's the way it was.

And is.

And ever more shall be.

But for an ending, yes, okay, let's not leave it there in the dismal environs of a city bus station. Let me rather bring things to a close in three steps: by minting another word, by thinking again about her ear, and finally returning to where I started: the two hairs fallen on my leg.

Word-minting (ii)

English is a wonderful language. However much I may sometimes bemoan the difficulty of finding the right words, I can usually find them eventually, or at least come close enough to what I'm aiming for to feel that I've managed to hit the target, even if not the bull's-eye. But despite its range, flexibility, and nuance, the way it lets us draw detailed maps of so much of the territory of human experience, there's no word for one of the most routine operations of the mind.

I'm talking about our daily looking at the world but not noticing what's there.

I don't mean by this any visual deficiency. Of course there are variations in the acuity of our vision, and the extent to which individuals can be considered observant varies enormously. But most people can see the things around them well enough, or if their vision is poor take steps to improve it. What I'm talking about is less easily recognized and corrected. I'm referring to our customary mode of engaging with the world — the everyday way we see and talk about things. This happens at a level of conventional convenience and superficiality that screens out much of what is there.

The truth is that the words English offers in such glorious profusion hide as much as they reveal.

I realize that language's strategic blinkering and omission are needed if it's to perform its essential function. If every name we bestowed unleashed the full nature of the thing it points to every time we uttered or wrote it, we'd soon be overwhelmed and lapse into silence, stupefied by

the gargantuan dimensions that edge all our sim-
plifications. The shorthand we rely on—*ear, girl,
hair*—allows us to screen out much of reality in order to navigate a way through it. Given the extent
to which, as a result, our outlook involves masking
as much as seeing, we might coin the term *seemask-
ing* as a way of referring to our customary way of
looking at the world. So, another definition.

> *Seemask* (verb): to look at the world but
> not really notice what's there; a kind of
> seeing-without-seeing. Seemasking is the
> accustomed gear at which we cruise
> through the everyday. Unless we get stuck
> in it, mistake seemasking for reality, this
> mode of perception isn't problematic;
> it's simply a practical way of dealing with
> things without troubling ourselves un-
> duly about their true nature.

Normally I'd just have seemasked the Australian girl's ear, looked at it through a perceptual
lens that's ground and dimmed by the silt of habit
and custom. I'd have glanced at it long enough to
label it as *ear* and then moved on to other things—
not really seeing it at all. But for some reason this
usual dynamic of noticing-yet-not-noticing failed
to kick in. Instead, her ear struck me in a radically
different fashion.

Ear (v)

As she braided her hair and dabbed patchouli
on her neck when she got up this morning, what
sounds were pouring into the ear that so entranced me? When she goes to bed tonight, what
will be the last sounds her waking mind is aware
of? What ancient dream sounds will sleep awaken

in her psyche? Does she ever think of the labyrinthine route through time that led her to the present moment, the incredible cargo of sounds — and sights and smells — that it contains?

How did she react when she first heard the three syllables of *genocide* uncoil their terrible weight of meaning into the depths of her listening?

When *God* is spoken, how does her brain decode that sound?

If *evolution* falls upon her ear, what images are conjured?

What does she feel when she hears the wind rushing through the trees, when her father calls her name?

How does she read the music of existence?

I don't know why, but as I looked at her ear it felt as if I was forced to eavesdrop on a whole range of questions, as distinctly evident, if not audible, as the words of her conversation with the woman who'd sat beside her on the bus.

The Australian girl drifts across my horizon of notice for a half-hour journey, then is gone for good. All that I'd like to have asked her remains in the realm of the unsaid. How does she face life and love and loss? What does she think and feel and dread? How does she understand our brief moments here beneath the stars, our brains assailed by the billion sounds that pour into our ears, the billion sights that pour into our eyes? Beyond life's cornucopia of sensation, can she see any sense?

I can infer some tentative answers by edging over that precarious bridge we cross so often: the shaky timbers the imagination lays down between self and other, now and then, and here and there.

But crossing it gives no guarantee of reaching the other side; it's a bridge that can turn back upon itself.

Enshrining the Hair of Strangers (ii)

I think again of the two hairs fallen on my leg.

But I picture them now as pieces of the umbilicus of time on which the present so depends. Along their length I imagine the text of this essay microscopically engraved, one word following another in a long continuous strand, a fragment of the DNA of expression with which we sculpt our voices into sounds that net things with their naming.

Yet for all the power of language, it's defeated in the end. These two fallen hairs are like gigantic versions of the tiny filaments that line the cochlea's inner seas, fishing there for sense. But when I stop and really listen to what they hook from the waters of the world, I'm left astounded by the nature of their catch and by its sheer improbability.

What are the chances that time should have been so torqued and shaped that it fell into the patterns needed for the three of us to coincide at these precise coordinates of time and space?

Is it not incredible that the long line of humans and prehumans stretching back from each of us should have so meandered that we came to be alive, in just this form and shape, for them to have their conversation, and for me to overhear it?

Think what a girl's exposed left ear reveals, even to a rudimentary timescan.

Be amazed.

Realize that these fallen hairs are tokens of something so shimmering with wonder that a shrine would seem the proper place to put them.

Voice Box

The drawer in which the oddments were stored had its own signature aroma. It's perhaps because of this—the fact that they were all bathed in the same enveloping smell—that I came to associate one thing with another, thought of them as a group, to the extent that some almost lost their individuality. This meant that for years the butterfly-wing cigarette box scarcely existed for me as a separate entity. I saw it merely as an integral part of this ragtag collection of things my father no longer had a use for but evidently still wished to keep. It was a long while before the box came into focus as the one unique object that speaks to me now.

I can summon the oddment collection's special odor back to mind pitch-perfect, but of course it's impossible to convey in words the exact heft and swirl of its olfactory contours. All I can do is provide the flat matter-of-factness of a list. The main ingredients were soap powder, wool, leather, rubber, cork soaked in whiskey, charcoal, antiseptic, and tobacco.

The drawers underneath the one that held the collection were filled with clothes, thus the notes of wool and soap powder. The oddments themselves accounted for the rest. Throughout my childhood, the scent that was released each time the drawer was opened spoke to me in a gruff adult voice that seemed at once to beckon yet warn of trespass, as if saying, "Look, here's an intriguing world—but you have no business in it. Keep Out!"

What was in the collection?

A leather holster for a service revolver; a gas-mask, its rubber perishing, the filter cracked open to reveal the charcoal lining; a field dressing, still in its original packaging, with "This side next to wound" in faded block letters; a regimental cap badge; three spent bullet cases; and a tin water bottle swathed in khaki felt and fitted with canvas carrying straps. Alongside these obviously military items there were two sturdy flasks for spirits, their glass sheathed in metal and leather, their shiny screw caps lined with cork. A faint suggestion of whiskey was detectable if you put them right up to your nose, though whether this was an actual remnant of the liquor they once contained or an imagined ghost scent, I'm not sure. There was also a black bowtie; a pair of elegant grey suede gloves; an assortment of cufflinks; a dented metal cigarette lighter; and finally the butterfly-wing cigarette box. It was empty, but its wooden lining still retained a breath of tobacco sweetness whenever it was opened.

This trove of aromatic oddments had been expelled from my father's personal territory — his desk, the drawers below the wardrobe in his room, his metal deed-box. Instead, it languished in a kind of exile, marooned in the no-man's-land of a tallboy on the landing. It was as if he'd set aside this period of his life — pre-marriage and prechildren — and placed it under a kind of house arrest or quarantine, a temporal apartheid that ensured the segregation of past and present.

As a boy, it was the accoutrements of war that made the most impression on me, particularly the gasmask and the leather holster. If you'd asked me then to describe the cigarette box, my response would have been sketchy at best. I'd probably have said it was a small silver-colored metal box with wooden lining, a rectangle of glass set into the lid, and behind the glass the rich blue iridescence of butterfly wings.

That the blue is background sea and sky for a picture of a ship is something I feel sure I must have noticed. How could I not have? But if I did, this crucial detail slipped out of mind. This meant that I was taken aback when, for the first time in years, I looked at the box again the other day and saw a ship in what I'd remembered as unbroken blue. Against what was held in my memory, the ship seemed like an intruder—an alien craft that had somehow slipped without permission into the territorial waters of my recollection and dropped anchor there, disrupting the image I'd misremembered for so long.

I like to think I saw the ship and then forgot about it. To have missed it altogether would suggest a worrying blindspot. But the way our gaze falls upon the world is far from straightforward. We select—and omit—as well as see. Our observation is quite different from any simple camera-like capture of what's there. Unlike the ship, though, I think I did simply fail to notice throughout my boyhood a feature of the box I spotted when I looked at it anew. I could have sworn there was no writing on it. But looking at it now I see a name faintly printed just below the picture of the ship.

It reads, *T.S.S. Vandyck.*

That name immediately recalled a series of pictures in one of my father's photo albums. In a section headed "Cruising 1938, *T.S.S. Vandyck,*" there are ten pages holding nearly fifty black-and-white photographs. Finding the ship's name on the butterfly-wing cigarette box made me pull out the album again and study this cluster of images more closely than I'd done before. A few names are written under photographs of the places visited: Madeira, Casablanca, Rabat, Lisbon, each one spelled out in my father's careful hand. But more interesting to me than any of these ports of call are the unlabeled photos taken on the *Vandyck* itself. The pages that they're on are simply captioned "On Board," with no further indication of who any of the people pictured are. The only one I recognize is my father. He looks tanned, relaxed, and younger than I know he must have been when the camera caught his smile in 1938 (thirty-three). He's almost always in the company of a strikingly attractive young woman. She's in so many of the "On Board" photos, and in most of those taken on sightseeing trips ashore too, that it's clear she was his main interest on that cruise.

Who was she?

What was their relationship?

At this remove in time I can only hazard tantalizingly uncertain answers.

If these were contemporary pictures, the way they are in each other's company would suggest that they were lovers. One photo shows them sitting snuggled up on two sun-loungers drawn close together on the deck. My father leans against her, his head nestled closely into her neck and shoulder. In another they're sitting on a rug spread out in a secluded corner of the deck. They're pulling each other into a tight embrace. She's in a sun-top, my father's wearing only shorts and white canvas shoes with the tops of oddly patterned socks visible at his ankles. Her arm is draped easily around his naked shoulders, her hand reaching down to cup around a bicep. He clasps her just above the waist so that the warmth and weight of her right breast must have been evident against his hand. There's a picture of them sitting together in a corner of the ship's swimming pool, legs entwined, and one where they're sunbathing on deck, my father leaning his bare back against her swimsuit-clad torso.

Two photographs of them taken singly are, to me, as suggestive of their togetherness as those where they're touching. Each of them in turn sits on the railings of the deck and smiles to the camera as the other — it seems reasonable to assume — takes the photo. They sit in exactly the same place, adopt the selfsame position and pose, resulting in his and hers portraits that you could imagine enlarged and framed and hanging side by side on the wall of a room in a family home, familiar domestic icons to the children growing up there. There's something relaxed and companionable in their expressions, yet complicit too. The way they gaze into the lens makes it hard to dismiss these or the other photos as evidence only of some passing flirtation.

But this is 1938, not now. I don't know what the sexual mores were back then. It's obvious they're attracted to each other. But eighty years ago would that attraction have been allowed the same expression it would find today? Was it just an innocent onboard liaison that meant little, led nowhere, no more than a holiday infatuation? Perhaps their poses of intimacy were really a kind of theatricality — playacting for the camera — a socially sanctioned expression of mutual attraction rather than an indication that anything of any consequence took place. Looking back over such a long period, it's hard not to smuggle into the perspective elements of a present-day point of view, and that may import currents of interpretation that don't correspond at all with the flow of what actually transpired aboard the *T.S.S. Vandyck* eight decades ago.

I've come to think of her as Zelma, though I've no idea if this was who she really was. Nor do I know much about Zelma in any case; so even if my naming of her thus is accurate, it doesn't get me much further. Every year at Christmas, without fail, a card arrived addressed to my father alone. The handwriting, fluent, almost bold, with an eye-catchingly well-balanced angularity, was always in the same blue-black ink. It was instantly recognizable, exuding an individuality that set it apart, an exotic foreigner amidst the run-of-the-mill cards from friends, family, and neighbors. Inside the card, beneath the printed Season's Greetings, was written "with my love, Zelma," followed by the *x* of a single kiss. If I asked who

Zelma was, my mother always replied, "An old girlfriend of your father's." She spoke with a mixture of admonishment, mockery, and resignation. Her tone did not invite further inquiry, nor for many years was I particularly interested in my father's life pre-me: the idea of parents having their own independent existence as individuals is an alien concept in childhood. By the time I was older, I suppose the cards from Zelma had become such an accustomed part of Christmas that I didn't think to question them. Zelma remains as mysterious, as unknown, as the young woman on the *Vandyck* whom she may, or may not, have been.

The *T.S.S.* (twin screw steamship) *Vandyck* was built in Belfast by Workman, Clarke & Company and launched on February 21, 1921. At that time my father would have been sixteen and on the point of moving from his family home in Londonderry to Belfast, where — except for wartime — he'd work for the rest of his life. Perhaps he attended the public spectacle of the launch, an event that always draws the crowds. He would certainly have read about the ship's completion in the local newspaper.

The shipbuilders who made the *Vandyck* were known locally as "the wee yard." But though less well known than Harland and Wolff, Belfast's famous industrial giant, the nickname is misleading. Only fifteen years after its establishment in 1880, Workman, Clarke & Company had become the United Kingdom's fourth-largest shipbuilder. As well as building relatively modest ships such as the *Vandyck* — some thirteen thousand tons and designed to carry cargo and a maximum of seven hundred passengers — they built transatlantic liners for customers like Cunard. The First World War brought considerable expansion as they took on naval contracts. In 1918, the company was taken over by Northumberland Shipbuilding. When that company went into receivership in 1927, Workman, Clarke briefly resurfaced, only to cease trading in 1935.

The *Vandyck* was originally brought into service with the Liverpool, Brazil and River Plate Steam Navigation Company, a subsidiary of the well-known Lamport & Holt shipping line. She sailed on the New York to River Plate route with ports of call in the West Indies and Brazil. As well as this usual plying between North and South America, the ship made one voyage in 1922 for the Royal Mail Steam Packet Company, sailing from New York to Hamburg. Sometimes I try to picture the tracery of lines that her various sailings would have left upon the oceans, imagine the water permanently marked by her passing, but of course there's no such indelible tattoo of presence, no permanent visible record of the miles covered, the routes taken.

The sinking of her sister ship, the *Ventris*, with the loss of more than a hundred passengers, coupled with the Wall Street Crash and subsequent worldwide depression, led to the *Vandyck* being taken out of service and laid up in the river Blackwater in Essex. This English waterway was dominated by laid-up shipping, particularly in times of economic downturn, with sometimes as many as forty vessels clustered together in a kind of commercial hibernation, temporarily mothballed, roosting until the economy summoned them to life again. When trading conditions began to improve in 1932, Lamport & Holt decided to refit the *Vandyck* for cruising. Pictures of the ship's dining saloon and lounges suggest considerable elegance. For her new role, the *Vandyck*'s hull was painted white, with a blue band running her full length just above the waterline, and a funnel banded in blue, white, and black. This is the livery in which she's shown in the picture on the butterfly-wing cigarette box. It's clear she was a sleekly handsome vessel.

Requisitioned by the Admiralty in 1939, the *Vandyck* was converted into an armed merchant cruiser. *H.M.S. Vandyck,* as she was renamed, was involved in the evacuation of allied personnel from Norway in the Second World War. During this operation she was bombed by enemy aircraft and sank in the Norwegian Sea off Andenes on June 10, 1940. Seven crew members perished. The remainder — around 160 men — abandoned ship and made it safely ashore, where they were captured by German forces.

Did my father or Zelma know what happened to the *Vandyck*?

It would surely not have surprised them to discover that it was claimed for military use. But I wonder if news of its sinking ever reached them. At the end of June 1940, the Registrar General of Shipping and Seamen in London wrote to the next of kin of those serving on the *Vandyck*. The letter informed them about what had happened and requested them to keep this information to themselves. One section of the letter reads:

> The circumstances in which the ship
> was lost do not permit of any public
> announcement being made at present
> and I have to ask that you will be good
> enough not to make known the fact that
> *H.M.S. Vandyck* has been sunk outside
> the circle of your immediate relatives,
> as it is not in the public interest that
> this information should be disclosed to
> the enemy.

The letter reassures recipients about the "very small" number of casualties, relatives of whom had been notified separately. For most, "there is no reason to suppose" that the husband, son, or brother in question "is not alive and well," since the majority of the crew "succeeded in landing in Norway." But the letter also warns of a less happy outcome, saying that "the possibility that they may have become prisoners of war cannot be overlooked."

It seems probable, in view of this effort to curtail dissemination of information, that few people at the time, apart from those directly affected, learned of the *Vandyck*'s fate. In any case, quite apart from the official decision to try to limit knowledge of what had happened, even if news of it had leaked out, it's unlikely that the sinking of one unimportant vessel, with relatively little loss of life, would have claimed much airtime or column space in those terrible years of conflict. By the time of the *Vandyck*'s sinking my father had enlisted and was serving with an artillery unit in North Africa. Amidst the sand and heat and gunfire in the desert, did he sometimes think of Zelma and their cruise? Did he ever discover that the railing they'd sat on to pose for photographs ended up fathoms below the surface of the icy waters off Norway?

If the lid of the butterfly-wing cigarette box is angled one way, the background to the picture of *T.S.S. Vandyck* looks dark and unexceptional. But tilt it slightly and the blue iridescence catches the light and glints magically, transformed into a striking azure sheen. The way the shimmer of the blue can be so easily made to come and go, as if switched on and off, provides a ready symbol for how the box can be read in different registers; how it appears according to two different ways of seeing. In one it seems dull, quotidian, easily contained within a routine description. In the other it becomes veined with the pulse and throb of voices telling a cluster of life-stories.

It's easy to list the raw factual details of the *T.S.S. Vandyck*: its tonnage (13,233 tons), length (510.6 feet), width (64.3 feet), depth (39.3 feet), number of cargo holds (5), capacity for passengers (300 first class, 150 second, and 230 third), maximum speed (14 knots), number of masts (2), funnels (1), date of launch (February 24, 1921), and date of sinking (June 10, 1940). In the same way, on a miniature scale, I could draw up a specification for the butterfly-wing box that presents it for scrutiny within a kind of descriptive scaffolding, a cage that holds it in place, confining details to the bare essentials:

> Metal alloy box lined with mahogany: 100 cm long, 90 cm wide, 53 cm

deep. Hinged lid—now broken—with
glass panel, behind which a ship is pictured, backed with the blue of butterfly
wings. *T.S.S. Vandyck* written in plain
font capitals in black along lower edge
of picture. *Made in England* stamped on
base. Twentieth-century souvenir cigarette box from a Lamport & Holt cruise
ship. Likely date of manufacture: 1930s.

Such a description may seem to bolt things
down to the stark, unaccompanied barebones of
their particularities. It is succinct, focused, and
gives us something clear-cut to hold on to. It acts
almost like a lifebelt that can be thrown into the
sea of complexities in which we swim, offering
the buoyancy of easy labelling without which we
would flounder. This kind of commonsense ap-
proach stops things from overflowing the channels
laid down by our ordinary diction; it blots out the
shimmer of the wings' blue mirror so that nothing
is reflected back except a handful of mundane details. But although it may possess a kind of superficial accuracy, this kind of description leaves out
so much that it also seems misleading.

Often, when I look at the butterfly-wing box
now, it seems like the entrance to a maze, a portal
giving access to a network of routes that beckon
me towards multiple unfoldings. Instead of its being something mute, it seems replete with voices;
instead of being empty, it seems to contain a dense
tangle of threads, as if countless Theseus-like
figures had unraveled their guiding lines through
this small section of history's labyrinth. One thread

leads back to my father's life, another to Zelma's and their 1938 cruise, whatever passed between them, the reason they went their separate ways, and what happened to them after they had parted.

But their two threads soon branch and interconnect and tangle with adjacent ones, become enmeshed in a plethora of other stories. Take a few steps in this direction and you'll find yourself in Belfast, in Workman, Clarke & Co's shipyard, maybe looking at the *Vandyck* planned out on paper, or maybe riveting sections of the hull together. Take a few steps in that direction and you'll be in Casablanca, on one of the ship's Mediterranean cruises. Follow this thread and it will take you to the offices of Lamport & Holt's shipping line with all the administrative mechanisms for organizing cargo and passengers. One thread takes you to Brazil and the West Indies, another to a warplane, its crew poised to bomb a ship off Norway. Spin the compass of possibilities that's invisibly contained in this little box and the needle may indicate the captain's story, or that of the grieving family of one of the crew members who died when the ship was bombed. Spin it again and it may point to the sufferings of the engineer held prisoner of war for years, or to whoever caught the South American butterflies whose wings still sheen the box's lid with blue.

The thread of the *Vandyck*'s history is interwoven with the lives of those who designed and built her, the stories of each crew member, all those who sailed in her, the dockworkers who loaded and unloaded cargo. Somewhere in this tapestry will be the thread of a lazy summer day, the ship at anchor on the Blackwater, a dragonfly

streaking across the oil-stained water, the sound
of cuckoos calling, and of Essex children playing
within sight of the river's load of laid-up vessels.
Somewhere there are all the nights at sea as the
Vandyck steamed along whatever itinerary it was
following, filled with its various cargoes and the
passions and secrets of its sleeping passengers,
their dreaming bodies lulled by the rhythm of
the waves. Somewhere there is the exact moment
the burnt-out hull touched the seabed when the
ship sank off the Norwegian coast. The box seems
less like something empty than a kind of conduit
through which surges a rich mix of narrative, the
blood of circumstance as it flows around the particularities that constitute what happens. Like any
object, the butterfly-wing box is part of history's
circulatory system—a capillary through which
time is channeled.

This souvenir cigarette box, emblazoned with
its picture of the *T.S.S. Vandyck*, once sat brand
new with others on a display shelf in a shipboard
shop, periodically lifted and examined for possible purchase by various now-long-dead passengers. How many weeks did it sit there before my
father bought it? Or did Zelma buy it for him as a
gift? For how many nautical miles did it sail before it went ashore with him? And what routes
did it take on land before it ended up in that tallboy drawer? How many hands have held it? What
conversations has it witnessed? What spectrum of
thoughts has it prompted?

Although the box bears on it the picture of
only one vessel, it sometimes seems more as if it

constitutes a kind of harbor thronged with craft and that the imagination is offered the possibility of embarking on any of them. Some will take it miles out to sea, across unfathomable depths; others will scarcely travel beyond sight of land. Each voyage represents one of the numerous lives that have been touched by this little trinket, a meteorite from 1938 now fallen into my keeping.

Like the *T.S.S. Vandyck,* laid up in the river Blackwater and then brought into service again, the butterfly-wing cigarette box was laid up for years in that tallboy drawer and then, after my father's death, in the backwaters of my own house until a chance discovery when I was clearing out the attic made me reconsider it. Now, this little box means more to me than I ever thought it would. Given its newfound significance, I find myself unsure quite what to do with it. Should I clean it up, display it somewhere as an ornament or curio, a conversation piece? Or just put it back in the dusty box in the attic beside the spirit flasks and cufflinks, part of my collection of oddments that no longer have any use? Perhaps I should make a pilgrimage to Norway, sail out from Narvik into the sea off Nordland County and drop it into the icy waters beneath which lie the remnants of the vessel that it pictures. I imagine it sinking through the fathoms to settle on the deck where my father and Zelma once basked in the Mediterranean sunshine. But such a gesture, however much it might promise something not unlike resolution, also seems a bit too melodramatic to seriously consider undertaking.

Instead, the line of symbolic harmony I've tak-
en, at least for the moment, has been to place the
box on a table on which are standing two now-
framed photographs, one of my father, one of Zelma, as they sit on the railings of the *Vandyck*'s deck
smiling for each other and the camera. And the box
is no longer empty. In it there's a memory stick.
Its files hold the text of this essay and scans of all
Dad's photos from that 1938 cruise. Filling the box
with this cargo and placing it between these two
images feels appropriate, apt, perhaps even mean-
ingful. But it could also be dismissed as merely rit-
ualistic, a foolish sentimental gesture that's obedient to the thirst for the kind of human symmetries
the world has little place for, something shamanic,
superstitious, without any respectable connection
to rationality. I readily confess that I don't know
how to determine whether the sonar of such actions pings back a sounding suggestive of significance, or if its haunting, searching note fingering
through the fathoms of history that surround us
locates nothing, but simply registers the echo of
what we want to find rather than the solidity of
something that's there independently of the de-
sires and fears that shape us.

Leaf

I'm often struck by how little it takes to set off a chain of associations in the mind. The smallest stimulus will do. So long as it's shaped and weighted to just the right degree, it can trigger a response whose scale completely dwarfs it. I'm sure there's an intricate array of biochemical processes in our brains that accounts for the way in which these large-scale concatenations are set off by the tiniest of prompts. But I find it hard to imagine beyond the haziest abstraction the elegant interlocking of cells and the microscopic transactions they broker; the chemical messages passed between them and the firing of nerve synapses as the mind's currents spark and flow. The invisible complexities that sustain us don't easily lend themselves to metaphor-making—our fundamental technique for bringing the world to heel and picturing it into sense. As George Steiner puts it, metaphors offer "new mappings of the world"; they lay down paths that we can follow in "our habitation of reality," making that habitation seem something familiar and intelligible. For all that they explain us, the unseen processes within are poor sources of imagery for the metaphorical cartography that helps us feel at home.

The way I've come to think of these periodic floodings of the mind—how it can be filled in an instant with a burgeoning network of connections—is to see the dam walls of consciousness as only *just* managing to contain what lies behind them. Reservoired in the invisible honeycomb that walls the psyche are huge volumes of life-water, categorized, corralled, confined, but always ready to escape. All it takes is that key last straw to break the back of restraint, to unlock a cell door, or to make permeable for a moment previously impassable walls, so that a deluge can pour out and cascade through the mind, causing one thought to lead to another.

Despite their scale, we are not swept away by such occurrences, and any sense of flooding they may cause is only temporary. Nor are our memories emptied of the loads of life-water that they carry, however much pours out. As such, instead of thinking in terms of escape from imprisonment, perhaps it would be more accurate to picture our consciousness as being swept by tides that are governed by the countless moons of circumstance with which we are surrounded. The ebb and flow of these inner tides depend on the complex gravity exerted by things, people, and events as they wheel in their tangled orbits around us.

The leaf that blew into the driveway of my house one October morning might seem an unlikely source of gravity — indeed an unlikely candidate for anything much, except whatever small-scale signaling of autumn it might manage. In fact, it exerted a powerful tidal pull. Or, to return to the picture of imprisonment in a honeycomb of cells, it was precisely one of those key last straws, possessed of far more backbreaking, unlocking, making-permeable potential than its ordinariness suggested.

I recognized the leaf's shape at once and

picked it up. As I did so, a welter of memories, associations, and ideas came flooding into mind. It seems incredible that such a tidal surge could have been summoned by so small a thing. But I can see no other obvious cause for it. This single fallen leaf, for all its seeming insignificance and fragility, somehow embodied in its shape and color, in its weight and texture, precisely the right launch codes to fire the sequence of associations that were set off in my mind the moment I found it.

Instantly identifiable because of its unique shape, the leaf was from a tulip tree (*Liriodendron tulipifera*). Sometimes tulip tree leaves are described as being "saddle-shaped," or looking as though their tips have been cut off with shears, or as having "four lobes and a flattened top." But such passive descriptions don't convey much unless you already have a picture of the leaf in  mind. If you don't, it's more effective to perform a small imaginative exercise. Think of a semicircle, its rounded side facing down. Then, on top of it, as if it was the start of a child's drawing of a boat, place a thick funnel, set dead-center, amidships. Now push the funnel down so that the straight line across the supporting deck of the semicircle is depressed in the middle, thus slightly raising either side and consequently emphasizing the points at bow and stern. Next, push down on the funnel's flat top so that it becomes dented into a *V* shape. Of course there are variations from tree to tree in

terms of the funnel's height and width, the extent
to which the points are uplifted, the overall size
of each vessel, and so on, but here essentially you
have it (once a stem is added to the curved base):
a tulip tree leaf's odd four-pointed form. No other
tree has leaves that fit this outline. It's a foolproof
way to recognize the species.

Liriodendron tulipifera is not a native tree in
Britain, nor is it common here. It grows to a considerable height, so it's not often found in people's
gardens. If the leaf that had blown into my driveway had been from an oak or beech or birch—
or any of the other common tree species—it's
unlikely it would have caught my eye. But for
me, *Liriodendron tulipifera* is something exotic, only
occasionally met with—added to which I happen to find it a particularly beautiful tree. It's not
surprising, then, that I'm predisposed to notice it.

The impact exerted by this single leaf, in terms
of setting off a chain of associations in my mind,
no doubt came about in part because of my liking
for this species, and in part because my encounters
with it have been few enough to make it seem fea-
sible to remember them. Prompted by the leaf, it
was as if all those encounters fell into line, forming
a kind of contour of recognition that marked out
a gentle gradient of remembrance that was easy
to follow. A similar mapping of, say, birch, would
have been quite different. My meetings with this
commonest of trees have been so numerous over
the years that they would soon generate a tangle
of contours. It would be difficult to map a way
through their dense complexity, easy to feel lost
amidst the whorls and blizzards of all the multitude of birch-lines. Quite apart from the fact that

birch flourished in the hedgerows and woods in the County Antrim countryside of my childhood, we often climbed a large silver birch that grew in our back garden, sometimes made tree houses in it, cut its branches to make spears and bows. To me, birch is so utterly familiar as to be hard to notice; it wears the camouflage of the known.

This exotic fallen leaf, blown into my driveway — the only one of its kind in the vicinity — acted like a kind of tuning fork. As soon as it sounded its characteristic tone, a cluster of voices answered, singing out in the same key reminders of their presence and strengthening the sense of a Liriodendron note resonating through me.

Here's an example of a truth that's easily forgotten, brushed under the carpet of our attention because of its very omnipresence: for all that we live together, sharing countless commonalities, for all that we successfully communicate with one another using the same vocabulary with its agreed range of meanings, we yet read the world in profoundly different ways, even when it comes to as small and apparently simple a thing as a leaf. I know that most people passing by my driveway that morning would have paid it no attention. For them, the leaf-song that I heard would have been inaudible. Anonymous participation in the crowd scene of autumn, a whispered contribution to its background rustle, would have been the only sound they might have credited to this single leaf. And even if it had stopped others in their tracks as it stopped me in mine, the leaf would have triggered in them a different cascade of associations, set in a different key, tuned to melodies I wouldn't recognize.

In one sense, yes, of course, a leaf is just a leaf. But in another, it possesses numerous facets of possible implication and interpretation. It has the potential to call up quite different catalogues of encounter, to spark an enormous variety of ideas and set free in the psyche an unpredictable diversity of images. It speaks to those who hear it in the argot of their individual experience, calling up the secrets of those specifics that unfold into — and that constitute — our different lives. Like almost everything, the leaf can tap into different strata of seeing. It can be read on the surface, according to the lexicon of the straightforward, those bold, block capitals that brook no ambiguity and dismiss any syntax of subtle complexities as unnecessary complication. Or we can delve deeper and read in a way that calls up far more finely textured scripts. On the one hand, the leaf is just a tiny pennant of autumn, insignificant in itself, its individual livery scarcely noticed — just one among billions of bits of fallen leaf-bunting that form en masse a routine semaphore of the seasons' turning. On the other hand, it's a kind of unique heraldic flag laden with mysterious insignia that are heavy with the weight of meaning coded into them — a weight whose tonnage is disguised by the featherweight, which is all that's evident when it's held balanced on the palm.

Finding the fallen leaf prompted me to make a kind of rapid inventory, ticking off on the register of remembrance the instances that together define my relationship with tulip trees. But although they form the bedrock on which my sense of *Liriodendron tulipifera* is founded, these memories are, I think, the least interesting part of the story, so I'll simply mention them quickly before passing on to what they point to.

The first tulip trees I'm aware of seeing were in Ireland, in the grounds of Ashford Castle, near the village of Cong in County Mayo. I didn't know then what they were but was immediately struck by their beauty. They lined both sides of a wide graveled path within sight of Lough Corrib, the massive lake (the second largest in the country) beside which the castle stands. I was sufficiently taken with them to make a point, on my return from County Mayo, of consulting a book of trees to try to put a name to what I'd seen. The task of identification was made straightforward by matching the oddly shaped leaf against a series of silhouetted leaf outlines given in a key.

Three or four years after seeing the Ashford Castle trees, my wife and I were in a very different part of Ireland, visiting my mother in County Antrim. One afternoon we walked to a garden center near where she lived in Lisburn and found a small *Liriodendron tulipifera* for sale. My mother bought it for us as a gift and we took it back to where we were living in Wales. The tree was small enough to sit on the floor behind the driver's seat of our modest hatchback. Its uppermost shoot only came to within six inches of the car's roof and none of the branches stretched out far enough to need bending in order to fit in. I can't remember now which of the ferries we traveled back on. Mostly we used the short Larne-to-Cairnryan crossing and then drove south to Wales through Scotland and England. But occasionally we drove to Dublin and took the longer sea-crossing from there direct to Holyhead in Wales. Whichever route we followed, when I think of the tulip tree in transit on the Irish Sea, it makes the ferry seem like a kind of giant pod and us its accomplices in a complex system of seed dispersal.

We were particularly pleased to be able to plant a tulip tree in our garden in Lampeter, a small town in rural west Wales that had grown up around St. David's University College, the institution where higher education had begun in Wales in 1822, and where I worked as a lecturer for many years. Shortly after moving there, we were reminded of how lovely tulip trees are when we discovered the beautiful one that grows just outside the college library. It was the only one for miles around. Indeed, in all the time we spent in Wales I don't remember seeing another in the area. It felt good, given this rarity, to be able to nurture a second specimen of our own. Our tulip tree flourished and soon became a striking feature in our garden, a familiar barometer of the seasons and a kind of slow chronometer of our lives. Every spring we delighted in the gradual unfurling of its new green leaves and watched as their fresh succulence darkened and toughened as summer progressed until, come September, the foliage started to display its warm autumnal palette of yellows, golds, and browns. When we planted it we had no children. By the time we left Wales, the tree was thirty feet high and had borne on its branches the weight of our two daughters and their friends. They climbed it, made tree houses in it, and built dens on the ground beneath it, cool in the shade it offered against the August sun.

One of the sadnesses of moving is that you can't take a garden with you. Leaving the one we'd created in Wales was far more of a wrench than leaving our house there. We took cuttings from many of our favorite plants when we relocated to Scotland in 2010. But the climate so much farther north was testing, and the soil conditions were very different, so few of them survived. With the tulip tree, in any case, though we were extremely fond of it, we made no attempt to propagate a new sapling. We doubted the wisdom of trying to grow so large a tree in our new, relatively small garden. As a memento, one sunny afternoon just before we left, I photographed our tulip tree in its early autumnal splendor. I deliberately zoomed in close enough so that the shot showed only a medley of green leaves streaked and patched to give a beautiful dappling of glinting yellows daubed with gold and brown. Using this image as a screensaver on my computer has meant having a daily reminder of the tree we felt we'd abandoned. I've often wondered since if it's still there, or if the new owners of the property decided it shaded the garden too much and had it felled. If it's left to flourish, it would be interesting to go back in ten or twenty years and see what size it is. There are reports of Liriodendrons reaching close to two hundred feet in their native American woodlands, though seventy to a hundred feet is commoner. It's incredible how much can be stored in a tiny seed—as it is to think that we once transported in our car, as a potted sapling, what became so grand a tree.

Finding an unexpected tulip tree leaf lying

windblown in the driveway of my house in Scotland inevitably made me think of the trees at Ashford Castle, the tree outside the college library
in Lampeter, and the one that we'd transported
across the sea from Ireland to our garden in Wales.
But such obvious memories, sewn into the weave
of personal encounter, didn't just present straightforward pictures of a handful of trees standing in
solitude, isolated from other aspects of experience.
Instead they came laden with images of the people, feelings, places, and events that I associated
with them, as if the Liriodendron's branches were
encrusted with a densely woven overlay, the coral
of my personal circumstances. As well as prompting such textured recall, the leaf also reminded me
of what I knew about the species — a smattering of
information gleaned along the way as my liking
for the tree led me first to identify and then to find
out more about it.

   Liriodendron tulipifera — its Linnaean niche of
classification — is mostly a misnomer. It combines
the Greek terms for lily (*leirion*) and tree (*dendron*).
Tulipifera means tulip-bearing. *Dendron* is the only
part of the name that has any claim to accuracy.
In fact, for me it is particularly apposite given its
connection to *dendrite*. Dendrites are the tree-like
branchings of nerve cells along which synaptic
impulses travel. My found leaf clearly touched, or
acted as, a nerve, sending a multitude of impulses
racing down the veined network of mosaic inter-
connections in which it was set.

   I'm not sure why the lily association was first
forged, since the tree is neither related to lilies nor
similar to them in appearance. Perhaps the flowers
seemed lily-like to some long-forgotten observer

not much given to botanical accuracy. Or perhaps they weren't looking at the blooms in situ on the tree. As Edward Step points out in his classic field guide *Wayside and Woodland Trees* (1940), tulip tree flowers "when picked and placed in flat bowls resemble small water lilies." It's also possible that the creamy whiteness of the wood brought to mind a lily's paleness, or the fragrant sap struck someone as reminiscent of a lily's perfume. It could even be that the majestic stature of the full-grown tree, coupled with its undoubted elegance, suggested something regal, so lily was reached for as an emblem of Hera, queen of the Greek pantheon. There are all kinds of currents moving beneath the surface of the names we give things. Some are easily charted; we can see immediately what they stem from, where they take us. But with others it's uncertain what resonance our use of them awakens, what histories and tonalities of reference our utterances are keying into.

The tulip component of the tree's name has a better claim to plausibility. Usually, it's said to be derived from the shape of the flowers, though sometimes the leaves are also said to be tulip-shaped in outline. There's some degree of tulip similarity in both. And since the genus to which tulips belong is in the lily family, *Liliaceae*, a massive umbrella grouping of more than 3,500 species, it could be argued (though not, I think, convincingly) that lily acts as a kind of generalized cognomen for tulip such that its application to the tree gains some little credibility through whatever tulip similarity is allowed. But the truth is that, closely examined, the leaf and flower of a tulip tree declare their own uniqueness more than suggesting a close resemblance to something else. In any case, flawed and misleading though *Lirioden-dron tulipifera* may be, I like the sound and rhythm of the name. Liriodendron in particular has an appealing lilting lyricism. It's often how I think of tulip trees.

There are misnomers too among the tree's common names. *Yellow poplar, white poplar,* and *tulip poplar* all mislead. *Liriodendron* is not a poplar. It belongs to the magnolia family. It's probable that this frequent (mis)application of poplar arises because of the way a tulip tree's leaves move in the wind. Their extravagant fluttering, set off by the lightest breeze, their ever-ready shimmering mobility, recall the movement of poplars, whose leaves, like well-set rigging, catch every breath of wind in a kind of deft multiple checkmate, each leaf-sail billowing in instant response to whatever air currents attempt to check against it. Such ready leaf movement is not just attractive, it serves a purpose, too: increasing airflow through the foliage and helping to accelerate transpiration and the movement of water through the tree.

There are two species in the Liriodendron genus, the North American *Liriodendron tulipifera* and the Chinese tulip tree, *Liriodendron chinense*. American tulip trees—the variety I'm concerned with here—were first introduced to Britain in the seventeenth century; the Chinese variety didn't reach this country until 1901. It seems almost certain that *Liriodendron tulipifera* found its way across the Atlantic courtesy of a royal gardener. That's the view given unambiguously by John Evelyn in *Silva* (1662), his "Discourse of Forest Trees and the Propagation of Timber in His Majesty's Dominions," published by the Royal Society. According to Evelyn, the first Liriodendrons were brought to Britain by "John Tradescant, under the name of the tulip tree (from the likeness of its flowers)." Evelyn also remarks on the leaves being "of a very peculiar shape." Following the death of the elder John Tradescant (c. 1570–1638), we know that his son, also named John (1608–1662), was appointed to the same quaint-sounding post that his father had held under King Charles I, namely, Keeper of His Majesty's Gardens, Vines and Silkworms. Tradescant Jr. made various foreign expeditions, including at least one, and possibly as many as three, to Virginia. The purpose of these travels was "to gather up all raritye of flowers, plants, shells etc." The tulip tree was one of the "rarityes" he brought back.

Like the Gingko and Sequoia, the Liriodendron is a living representative of an ancient family. Tulip trees can be traced back for more than one hundred million years to the Cretaceous period. It's strange to see leaf fossils preserved in rock that appear identical to tulip tree leaves today and to realize that the one blown into my driveway is part of a species whose lineage reaches back to when dinosaurs still walked the earth. Tulip trees make our human tenancy of time seem only just begun. Looking at the fact that oak trees can take three hundred years to grow, three hundred years to live, and three hundred years to die, Robert MacFarlane has suggested in *The Wild Places* (2007) that "such knowledge, seriously considered, changes the grain of the mind." Looking at the Liriodendron's lineage, it feels more as if the mind's temporal grain has been snapped and broken, leaving it reeling with a sense of its own spectacular littleness.

As well as establishing their ancientness, the fossil record also shows that Liriodendrons once flourished over a much wider range than they do today. The fact that they died out in Europe was due to extreme climate change as the ice took hold. I like the fact that having planted a tulip tree in Wales I wasn't so much introducing an exotic species as reintroducing a native after an absence that lasted for eons. But what's a mere eon when measured on the chronology of a species whose bloodline — sapline — is so old, whose roots are sunk so deeply into time that it makes our human hold on it seem fleeting and precarious?

Canoe wood is another of the tree's common names, referring to the fact that Native Americans in the east of the country favored it for their dugouts. The large trunk size and fine grain of the wood made it ideal raw material for such vessels, which could hold ten or even twenty people. As well as boat building, the syllabus of human uses for the timber includes furniture, house construction, church organs, and coffins. Just as the leaves on the tree move readily in the slightest wind, so this single leaf fallen in my driveway seemed to shimmer in my hand, setting off a ripple of thoughts. It made me wonder about all the lovers who've lain in beds strutted with Liriodendron wood, all the corpses encased in it as they were lowered, coffined, into the earth, all the organ notes listened to by brides and bridegrooms, and by mourners, the air blown through pipes trimmed and set with this fine-grained timber. As we lie down to love, to rest, to die, we've often been cradled by this ancient timber, which so massively predates our hominid origins that it makes all our rites of passage seem but newly minted.

The leaf in my driveway had the power to bring back memories of the encounters I've had with tulip trees over the years, and to make me recall at least some of what I've read about this ancient species. But for me, the potency of this little piece of flotsam lay not so much in its predictable ability to summon into present consciousness what I already knew about it, the people and places I associated with it. It lay rather in its arresting otherness. When I picked it up, I could sense within the penumbra of the known something profoundly unknown. This made memory's reassuring handholds seem less like markers of something that I recognized more like flimsy camouflage around a mysterious core.

This fragile piece of nature's fabric, this little scrap of world-stuff, could command the mind's tides to run and turn, summoning and dismissing its waves. But it was the undertow, what the waves pulled me towards, not the waves themselves that left the strongest impression. Ashford Castle, our *Liriodendron tulipifera* transported to Wales from Ireland, details of the tree's name, appearance, size, and range — these are just ripples on the surface, white horses of the familiar. It's what lies below them that astounds — the deeps of time and space yawning just below the navigable leaf-shallows in which we paddle, safe in our dugouts of discourse, our route clearly marked by the buoys of vocabulary and all the reassuring proto-

cols of parlance. No matter how much we try to
mask and muffle it, balanced lightly on my palm
that October morning, weighing no more than a
feather, was part of the substance of things, the
stuff of reality, heavy with the coiled story lines
it carried.

As I held the leaf, gripping its stem tightly to stop it from blowing away, the wind gust-
ed strongly. Across the road from where I live
there's a school that has several flagpoles near its
entrance. The sound of lanyards rapping against
the metal poles immediately brought to mind
the oddly pleasing dissonance of the same sound
multiplied twenty times by vessels anchored in a
densely boated harbor, lines jangling against their
masts. I guess it's this which, for a moment, put
a nautical spin on things. For all its insubstantial,
featherlight presence, the fact that I could crumble
it between my fingers, the leaf also had the air of
an anchor to it. Straining against its hold, berthed
invisibly in its essence, lay the massive seagoing
vessel of a life-shape carved and repeated over
many millennia. In every twig, in every leaf — if we
listen carefully — there's an echo of Liriodendron's
voyage, its seeding and rooting, its growing and
flowering, its faltering and dying over millions of
years. Its signature foliage moves to the rhythm of
the seasons' cycles: from green to gold and brown
to bare branches and back to green again as each
tree, its leaf-canvas responsive to every nuance of
the weather, sails through time's waters.

Leaves in their number and fragility, their
short-livedness, are like us humans. It's as if they
put on a kind of annual mortality play — a vivid
memento mori — every autumn. But each individ-

ual tree in the Liriodendron clan also follows a kind of leaf-cycle life-cycle as it grows and flourishes and dies, settling back into the earth from whence it was drawn, its recipe of form and function dissolved back into the rich components of the generating—and degenerating—humus. Its elegant structure is dismantled and reassembled repeatedly. It's as if leaf and root and bark, the paleness of the wood, the fragrance of the flowers, are verses in some poem that the earth has learnt by heart and keeps reciting to itself over and over again across uncounted centuries, conjuring the trees into existence, forming and reforming them with repeated persistence.

A tulip tree doesn't flower until it's at least ten years old, often not until it's fifteen or more. Writing in *The Guardian* newspaper's blog in July 2012, John Lydon talks about waiting to see tulip trees planted outside Leeds University's Edward Boyle Library come into bloom and his "childish excitement" when, eventually, they do and he sees this long-anticipated sight for the first time in his life. The flowers are beautiful but discreet, easily missed amidst the foliage unless the tree is thickly covered in them, or unless—like Lydon—you've been watching for them carefully every year.

The first time I saw the flowers was when a sparse scattering of them appeared one summer on the tulip tree in front of the college library in Wales. Eventually, our own Liriodendron flowered, seventeen years after we'd planted that spindly sapling we'd brought across the sea from Ireland. By then it was nearly thirty feet high. This

long wait for the flowers confers a special quality of rarity on them; it adds to their specialness,
making them seem secretive, mysterious. What
decrees the time lapse between the tree's initial
germination and its flowering? What complex calibrations of wood and light and leaf, of water and
weather, of trunk girth and height combine to key
into the plant's chemistry the instruction to wait,
the instruction to blossom?

I like Edward Step's description of the flowers:

> They have oblong, greenish-white
> petals, which may reach one-and-a-half
> inches. There is an orange-colored spot
> at the base of the petal where nectar
> is secreted. The petals are erect, and
> have the tips overlapping, giving
> the flower the typical cup shape. The
> stamens, which are numerous, are
> crowded round the large and pointed
> central pistil. They are orange and yel-
> low in color. Although the individual
> flowers are somewhat inconspicuous
> when seen against foliage, the spectacle
> of a tulip tree in full flower is very
> striking, especially in moonlight.

I've never seen the flowers by moonlight and
hope I get a chance to before I die. There must
have been moonlit nights in my garden in Wales
when our tree was in flower, but at that point I'd
not read Edward Step and didn't think to look. No
doubt, returning late from college dinners, I may
even have walked down the path beside the tree,
oblivious to the spectacle above me. Seeing them
in daylight is enough to have convinced me of the
loveliness of the flowers, but I find Step's mention

of them in moonlight oddly evocative. It makes me wonder about all the members of my species, since our African emergence, who have gazed upon this sight, what they felt as they did so, what befell them, and how their stories and mine and *Liriodendron tulipifera*'s are sutured into the fabric of existence. How — why — did they begin? How do they relate and overlap? What endings do they move towards? And is there any sense to the patterns that all of us trace out upon time's capacious, mystifying canvas? As generations of us come and go, as we progress through our seasons, our bodies budding, flowering, and faltering, I find it at once comforting yet at the same time hauntingly elegiac to think of all those undocumented moments across the centuries when tulip tree flowers have caught the eyes of human watchers, sparking diverse chains of association in uncounted minds. I'm reminded of a line in William Meredith's "Accidents of Birth" where he talks about life "throwing its sensual astonishments upside down on the bloody membranes behind my eyeballs." A tulip tree in flower is surely one such "sensual astonishment" — and the fact that we have eyes to see it, that it is there to be seen during our brief moments of existence, seems the kind of sheer improbability that's hymned by Meredith in this wonderful poem about contingency.

Before synthetic materials replaced it, tulip tree wood was used in the manufacture of organs. Its fine grain means it can be cut with sufficient accuracy to stopper the instrument's pipes and valves and so channel and contain the air sent through them, doing so with sufficient precision to ensure reliable notes. When I discovered this

use for the wood, it made me wonder at the immense toccata and fugue that's played by *Liriodendron tulipifera*. The music of the tree is written into
every part of it, its notes encoded, like strands of
DNA, with the blueprint of its form, the history of
its existence, the fact of its being. Yet etched into
the scaffolding of the branches, the network of its
roots, the annual canvas of the leaves, the eventual
flowers, there's far more than the tulip tree's story,
fantastic though it is. In the places it has grown,
in the seasons it has weathered, in the eons it has
flourished, the trees stand witness to what passes
there, and we are part of that tapestry of intricate
happenstance, part of the crowded fabric of existence. As I hold the leaf and try to listen, I realize
that my ears are attuned to catch only the smallest
fragments of the music that it plays. My words can
make only millimetric incursions into the harmo-
nies of being that fountain out of the massed organ
pipes of Liriodendron's trunks and branches. I can
scratch the surface of what's there, but what sur-
renders to my clumsy notation gives only the most
superficial account. The Liriodendron's breathtaking yet elegant complexity, the stave of its ancientness, means that it plays at a pitch and pace that
I'm helpless to transcribe beyond the cartoon sim-
plifications of metaphor and narrative.

Think of all the tulip tree leaves that have ever
existed on this planet, each one hung on its twig,
arrayed on the tree's branches like notes on a score.
Imagine each one stirring in the wind, leaf striking
against leaf to produce a susurration that's more
oceanic than orchestral in its scale and volume.
Think of all the insects that have moved across the
millions of leaf-acres so constituted, the rivers of

rain fallen on them, think of every creature, from dinosaur to human, that has stood in the shade of a Liriodendron, of every footprint on the ground beneath their shading branches. The impossibility of properly describing sits just below the surface of our diction. Sometimes our ordinary accounts of things, the stories that we tell, seem like the thinnest of integuments draped over an abyss. It does not take much to punch through an apparently simple statement like "I found a tulip tree leaf blown into my driveway" and end up floundering in what lies within it.

I have a tendency to pick up little keepsakes along life's way: pebbles, feathers, seashells, fir cones, leaves. I'm not sure I fully understand the impulse behind this beachcombing. In part, perhaps, it's a kind of collector's instinct, the desire to have and to hoard. But I don't want complete sets of things, systematically accumulated, in the manner of a dedicated collector. Rather, I'm drawn to serendipitous shards that happen to catch my eye just now and then. In part, I think such beachcombing is an attempt to acquire concrete reminders of times and places that will act like little doorstops, preventing forgetfulness from slamming shut memory's door too soon. But more than obeying these collecting and souvenir-gathering imperatives, I think I'm driven simply by a kind of stupefied amazement at the nature of things. I want to have tokens, tangible mementos, which remind me of the nature of the real. For we so often swathe things in a cladding of the quotidian, blinker our vision so that it's focused on those commonsense perspectives that are of course necessary for day-to-day living, but that can take on an obscuring permanence if we're not careful, make us forget what lies beneath them. Things like the tulip tree leaf seem somehow bladed; they act like scalpels, cutting away the commonplace. Through their incisions we can catch glimpses of a different order of being to the one we usually inhabit.

Little keepsakes is a misleading locution, both in terms of its suggested scale and in its implied promise of permanence. The tulip tree leaf may be small enough (six inches from bow to stern, four-and-a-half inches from the *V* of the funnel to the start of the stem), but it's inextricably implicated in much more gigantic scales. Even without touching on its genesis and evolution, it buys into the process of photosynthesis, upon which life on Earth depends. As a February 2, 2013 article in *New Scientist* puts it, "you have photosynthesis to thank for every lungful of air you breathe." And as for keeping the Liriodendron leaf, it won't be for long. This keepsake will sit on my desk for a while, but it will soon be lost or forgotten or just get damaged and thrown away. Like us, it isn't made for permanence. Were it not for the special extra-somatic memory that writing creates, preserving the leaf in the amber of these sentences, I'd probably have forgotten about it already.

I used to press occasional leaves and wildflowers in a massive family Bible, thick and heavy as a headstone. It came from the County Antrim farm on which my mother and her sisters grew up and had, before that, belonged to her grandfather. No one seemed to know its age or provenance beyond that. The Bible was used more as a depository than a book. Between its thick, parchment-like pages, each one as large as a poster, there was a rich scattering of what others had left behind over the years: news cuttings (mostly obituaries) that were yellowed and brittle with age; spindly remnants of wildflowers, their blooms almost transparent, leached of all but the most dilute trace of color; exam certificates; letters; and, my favorite, what we used to call *skeleton leaves,* leaves where almost all of the connective tissue had gone, leaving a lacework scaffolding of midrib, outer edge, and veins, a kind of ghost leaf, the tracery of form still evident, a fugitive whisper of vanished substance.

If I'd still had the family Bible — more slab than book, a leather-covered monstrosity that I passed on to a cousin when I moved house, not wanting to add its weight and bulk to the complications of moving — I'd have pressed my tulip tree leaf in it. That way I might have stayed the hand of disintegration for a while, ironing out the wrinkles, fixing by the weight of the pages its shape and color. As it was, even just thinking of pressing it brought the family Bible back to mind — another part of the flood of associations set off by the leaf.

A Bible holding pressed leaves between its pages offers a striking symbol for the way in which the evolution of writing is closely connected to plants. Leaves were among the earliest surfaces on which we incised our script. Palm leaves, for example, were the medium for early Sanskrit, and the very name of paper comes from that most famous Nilotic reed, papyrus. Scholars have pointed to the way in which book and tree go hand in hand. For example, in *Beyond the Written Word* (1987), William Graham notes that:

the word for "book" in English and its cognates in other Germanic languages (as the German *buch*, Dutch *boek*, or the Swedish and Danish *bok*) have commonly been linked etymologically with the name for beech tree (Old Norse bók, Old English *bók*), the bark or wood of which may have been the earliest form of writing material among Germanic peoples.

Reverse and obverse pages are still called leaves, and the double page of a ledger is called a folio (from folium, a leaf). When we say "leaflet" now, it's unlikely our first thought will be "little leaf," but the word again emphasizes the writing–leaf connection. In this age of electronic text and screens, we may have cut the umbilical between them, but laid down in the very etymology of *book* and *paper* is evidence that something arboreal is a foundational part of the genome of our literacy.

The nineteenth-century Scottish writer Alexander Smith suggests in *Dreamthorp* (1863) that "the world is everywhere whispering essays and one need only be the world's amanuensis." But being the world's amanuensis is far from straightforward. How can we put into words the wonders that are routinely dictated to us? Thinking about fossil Liriodendron leaves laid down in rock, and leaves pressed in Bibles, about the leaf blown into my driveway, about what happens in photosynthesis and pollination, about invisible processes at a molecular level, invisible structures at an atomic level—all of it makes me imagine a thick tome made of tulip tree leaves, one oddly shaped leaf-page for each year of its existence from the Cretaceous to the present. And on the leaves of this massive volume, bound in the tree's pale wood, the incredible Liriodendron story, only hinted at here, could be written out in full. To decode what's carried by a tulip tree leaf and write about it within the compass of an essay is, inevitably, to act as editor more than amanuensis, radically cutting out; offering abstractions, excerpts, glimpses rather than anything approaching a faithful copying of the full text that we're given. A sense of how we might move closer to transcription can be gleaned from Jan Zalasiewicz's remarkable book *The Planet in a Pebble* (2010). Taking a pebble from a beach, Zalasiewicz shows that once we learn to decipher its cargo, the pebble, as his title suggests, contains no less than a history of the planet. His book is a master class in how extraordinary the ordinary things around us are. It suggests how we might at least begin the process of transcribing all that's written in a leaf.

The windblown leaf I found in my driveway was like a kind of letter delivered by the season, a note from one small entry in our planet's register of life-forms. Written on it — in it — were details of stupendous spans of time, and of the intimate, intricate mechanics that have powered Liriodendron through them. Where had this particular leaf-letter come from? I can't be wholly sure, but so far as I know, the only tulip trees in the area are in the Botanical Garden quite near to where I live. There are several of them there, most a little larger than the tree we had in Wales. It provided a perhaps baseless sense of something fitting that at

one point in writing these lines I took my pen and
notebook and wrote while sitting on a bench under one of these trees. When I did so, I wasn't just
moved to think about all the other visitors to the
garden who had sat on this same bench beneath
the Liriodendron, its leaves stirring and whispering above them, or about the tree in starlight and
in rain, the bare branches sometimes powdered
white with snow. As well as imagining all this,
and the butterflies that had alighted on the foliage
to bask in the summer sun, as well as picturing
how the flowers might appear in moonlight, I also
remembered Pando.

Pando (which means "I spread" in Latin) is the
name that's been given to one of the largest and
oldest organisms on earth. Also referred to as the
"Trembling Giant," this life-form is thought to
weigh around 6,500 tons and to be at least eighty
thousand years old. To put that in some sort of
graspable perspective, an adult male blue whale
weighs around 150 tons (about the same as twen-
ty-five elephants), so Pando would be equivalent
to more than forty of such giant cetaceans. Going
back eighty thousand years takes us to the time of
our human exodus from Africa — when *Homo sapiens* left the cradle of its birthplace to colonize the
Earth.

Pando is a huge grove of quaking aspens,
spread over one hundred acres, which grows in
Fishlake National Forest in Utah. There are almost
fifty thousand individual trees, but *individual* is
not quite right. For each one of them shoots from a
single source, a massive underground root system.
Each tree is more like a leaf of one supertree than a
separate, different individual. The quaking aspen

(which belongs to the poplar family) is so called because of the readiness of its leaves to do precisely what a tulip tree's leaves do—stir and flutter in the slightest breeze. The scale and age of the Trembling Giant are humbling. But it's dwarfed by tulip trees with their Cretaceous pedigree. And though they may not occur as a single clump, a root mass easily identified as one, is it not true that they're all part of the same life-pattern, that my single fallen Liriodendron leaf is integral to something singular whose scale and age are hard to picture on the canvas of our ordinary apprehension, framed as it is by the kind of calibrations that cut things into the little measures we can fathom? Just as what's familiar can soon seem strange, so what's many can seem one; and relationships between things, the identity of things, slip into another gear and become less certain than it seemed before.

So much is written in so little that it can appear fantastical, as if we've stumbled on some kind of fairy artifact, something charmed and magical, imbued with special powers. A leaf unfurls, green and fresh, it grows to full size. It reaps its harvest from the sun, it's there in moonlight, rain, and wind. It takes on its autumnal color, falls from the tree, is blown away, lands in a driveway, and is picked up from where it's fallen. And in that isobar of small events, the little timeline of a single leaf, there are echoes of such haunting resonance that they allow us to glimpse massive vistas of time, heavy with the cargoes that they carry. Behind the paper-thinness of this one fallen leaf, its wafer-light familiarity, stands something wholly other—the brute, but beautiful, fact of existence. All of us are leaves on its enormous tree. The

mind's tides and seasons, like the flux of Liriodendron, like everything else around us, quake and
tremble in the astonishing winds of Being.

Letters

In the course of the coronavirus pandemic, during Scotland's first lockdown in the spring of 2020, we took to playing Scrabble again. One evening, instead of playing with our usual set, I got out the one that dates from my childhood. The main difference between the two is that the old set's letter tiles, and the little racks that hold them, are made of wood, not plastic, and the box they and the board fit neatly into is maroon, whereas our present one is green.

I hadn't handled the wooden tiles for years and it came as a surprise how different they feel to the plastic ones, despite their identical function. Their smooth, cool solidity generates a sense of intimate precision. They seem closer to tracing out the actual shapes of the designated letters. The wooden tiles have a weighted exactitude that's absent in the plastic ones. There's a miniature density to them that suggests the concentration of something distilled. Placing them recalls the fluency of calligraphy rather than the clunkiness of typesetting.

In my childhood, we only played Scrabble infrequently and, for my part, reluctantly. It wasn't something I found pleasure in for years. My parents viewed it as an educational activity more than anything to do with fun, something that would widen our vocabulary, polish our overall literacy, make us more adept with words. I don't know if it had any such improving impact on me. I certainly wasn't a natural at it, and any increase in skill that came with practice was rendered imperceptible by the long gaps between our games. Perhaps being the youngest in the family was some excuse, but for an unconscionably long while it felt that I was stuck at the level of making short words of embarrassing obviousness. I watched in silence as my parents and brother forged clever links and connections that skillfully exploited what was on the board, conjuring obscure words that I had never heard of to achieve scores that made mine seem paltry even when the handicap of age was factored in.

Gradually I got better at it and started to enjoy the game. But for much of my childhood it was a penance. I was pleased that, for the most part, the Scrabble lay unused in its maroon box, stored in the bottom drawer of a mahogany tallboy. Neatly folded beside it were my mother's carefully ironed tablecloths, tea towels, and napkins. This meant that the smell of starched linen pervaded everything kept in the drawer. Even now, all these years later, a ghost of that scent still clings indelibly to the Scrabble, so that when I opened the maroon box again it triggered a flurry of memories.

Maybe because my parents seemed traditional, old-fashioned in their tastes, not given at all to newfangled things, I used to think of Scrabble as something far more ancient than it is. For years I assumed they must have played it with their parents, and that their parents before them would likewise, in their turn, have been introduced to it by theirs, each generation initiated into playing by the one before. Though I didn't have a clear idea of an absolute beginning for this process of familial transmission, I imagined a hoary pedigree. It wouldn't have surprised me to discover a lineage stretching back to some rough-hewn proto-form invented by our cave-dwelling ancestors. Every family I knew possessed a set. That reinforced the sense of its being a long-established activity, a kind of universal. Scrabble was as much a household staple as a box of matches. Putting those wooden tiles together to make words seemed almost as elemental as rubbing sticks together to make fire.

My picture of the long history of family Scrabble playing is entirely wrong. The game isn't even a hundred years old. It was invented in 1933 by Alfred Butts, an unemployed New York architect. He initially called his new creation Lexico, then Criss Cross Words. Manufacture began on a tiny scale, as a cottage industry, with Butts making the games himself. As Stefan Fatsis notes in *Word Freak*, his study of the personalities and passions of competitive Scrabble — a world away from our low-key family games — sales were tiny to begin with. Fatsis records that Alfred Butts "gave a few sets to friends to test them out and then began selling them from home at $1.50. He sold two in October 1933, four in November, and nineteen in December." By August 1934, sales amounted to a grand total of eighty-four sets — far from enough to make a living.

Things changed when Butts met games enthusiast James Brunot, a former social worker keen to establish a business in his hometown of Newtown, Connecticut. But even with Brunot's dynamism driving things, production remained modest.

Brunot, his wife, Helen, and the small team they
assembled made 2,400 sets in 1949, a year after the
name they'd come up with, Scrabble, was trade-
marked. But even with 2,400 sets a profit eluded
them; they recorded a loss of $450.

Despite these uncertain beginnings, things
were poised to take off. The sequence of events
that's become a kind of brand creation-story has
it that a senior figure in Macy's department store
discovered the game while on holiday and subse-
quently ordered it for Macy's shelves. It caught on
and sold like hotcakes. Even taking on more work-
ers and running at full tilt, the Brunots' operation
could only make six thousand games a week, not
nearly enough to keep up with orders. To satisfy —
and further stoke — demand, they sold the licence
to produce Scrabble. It was bought by well-known
games manufacturer Shelchow and Righter, who
had the capacity to operate on a grand scale. They
sold eight hundred thousand Scrabble sets in 1953.
Public demand became insatiable. Shoppers who
wanted Scrabble as a Christmas gift had to put
their names on a waiting list. Our family's wood-
en-tiled Scrabble set has "Copyright 1954" printed
on the board. That was the year sales peaked, with
four million copies sold.

In the years since then, the rights to the game
have passed between various games manufactur-
ers as businesses were bought and sold. Current
ownership is split between Hasbro, who control
the rights to Scrabble in America, and Mattel, who
do so in the rest of the world. Today, it's estimated that some 150 million Scrabble sets have been
sold worldwide, across 121 countries, and that
the game has been translated into twenty-nine

languages. More than half of British homes have a Scrabble set. In the United States, it can be found in one out of every three households. Alfred Butts, the game's inventor, lived comfortably on the royalties he earned from sales and died shortly before his ninety-fourth birthday in 1993. James Brunot, who developed and renamed the game in those crucial early days, made an even larger fortune and died in 1984 at the age of eighty-two.

When it came to clearing their house after my parents' deaths, the set of wooden Scrabble surprised me with the strength of resistance it summoned against being thrown away. It was as if all the letter tiles arranged themselves into words commanding STOP whenever I considered binning them. An aura of protective preservation emanated from the Scrabble set; it whispered KEEP ME in my ear. At the time, I didn't give much thought to this invisible interdict. I just surrendered to it, somewhat sheepishly, because it felt that I'd given in to yet another irrational impulse to keep something. The Scrabble set was duly added to the pile of things being salvaged before the house was sold. For years it lay unused in the attic of my house. Anytime my family plays the game it's with our own plastic set. The old Scrabble is one of many items of memory-laden bric-a-brac that have no present function in my life, but that are so redolent of childhood they've retained a claim on my affections. No doubt this is an admission of lamentable sentimentality, of being in thrall to mere nostalgia, but I still don't feel inclined to jettison these material revenants.

I'm not sure what made me remember the old maroon box of Scrabble in the attic with its wooden tiles and racks, or why I got it out again that evening during lockdown. But I'm glad I did. Handling the wooden tiles, it felt as though my parents' voices had been reawakened; I could hear them again distinctly in my mind. I know the alphabet's *A* to *Z* is impersonal, capable of being used by anyone to say anything, and to say it in a multitude of tones and accents. But this box of wooden letters is so much a part of childhood that it feels as if it holds the fossilized traces of my parents' unique diction, rather than being just an anonymous trove of speech fragments that anyone might have spoken. These Scrabble tiles are like crystallized remnants of my parents' utterances, as if their words had been carefully disassembled into their constituent elements and salted down for safe keeping in the little seam of history that's held in the confines of the maroon box. Knowing that they'd held each tile, placed them with deliberation, used them to spell out on the board what was simmering in their minds, adds to this sense of presence. Spectral echoes of my parents cling to the wooden tiles as surely as the scent of starched linen. Playing with the old Scrabble doesn't make me remember any of the odd, disjointed combinations of words placed on the board in the course of our games. Instead, what comes back to mind is our conversation. This returns not as a verbatim transcript of what we said, but rather as a memory of the timbre of voices, the lilt and tone of our affectionate exchanges as we clustered around the fireside table, each with a rack of letters in front of us, on those long-ago winter evenings, the wind

howling outside, the rain loud against the win-
dowpanes.

I realize this may seem fanciful. That an old
set of Scrabble may be imbued with memories
sounds reasonable enough. But to present it as if it
offers some kind of magic mechanism of resurrec-
tion isn't credible. Nothing can restore the voices
of the dead. Yet for me, it acts in such a vividly
mnemonic manner it's hard not to exaggerate the
power it has to summon back what's gone. Whatever talismanic properties it may possess in terms
of prompting the recall of personal memories,
Scrabble has, without doubt, considerable power as a kind of lens or mirror that lets us see how
much we rely on the alphabet. Playing with the
wooden Scrabble tiles didn't just bring a raft of images from childhood back to mind; it also flagged
up the way in which we fish out of our shoal of
familiar letters the elements we need to put our
ideas into communicable shape. Scrabble makes
plain the extent to which everything that's spoken
and written depends upon this little catechism
of symbols. It's just a game, I know. But there's
also something about it that helps cast light on the
nature of our relationship with the alphabet and
how, without its twenty-six letters, we'd be unable
to bring meanings into focus and parse the world
with sense.

Having the letters of the alphabet marked out
individually on a Scrabble set's collection of tiles
presents a tangible expression of the rich poten-
tiality of language. Even with just the seven letters that each player picks out, there are all sorts

of possibilities. They can generate, according to
Stefan Fatsis's calculation, "3,199,724 unique combinations." Think of what all one hundred tiles
(ninety-eight letters and two blanks) could give
rise to. But although it can be thought of in math-
ematical terms, I find a different image comes to
mind. They may be simple, hard-edged objects
clearly separable from each other, but I've come to
think of Scrabble's letter tiles as something liquid.
They flow together, form a kind of pool, so that
instead of being discrete, solid entities they seem
more like the constituent molecules of a kind of
primordial verbal lava. They represent the way in
which language offers an infinity of raw meanings
held in a molten state of readiness, poised to gel
into whatever meanings we want to give form to
through words.

We use letters so routinely, have become so
accustomed to them, that it's easy not to notice
the alphabet's flexibility and reach. The malleabil-
ity and scope of letters is astounding. We can use
them to describe the feelings that are attached to
an old set of Scrabble, and to trace out the history
of the game. Or they can be tasked to map out the
age and structure of the Earth and its place in the
solar system. We can marshal them into lines of
verse, produce accounts of photosynthesis, write
about our terrors, hopes, and dreams, cast light
on other times and places, tell our diverse human
stories. In short, as Richard Firmage puts it in *The
Alphabet Abecedarium*, letters "enable the magic of
literary creation." By slowing down the process of
word-making, rendering it more self-conscious,
presenting it in miniature on the stage of the board
under the spotlight of the game, Scrabble makes

more obvious the enormous range of meanings we can conjure from just twenty-six symbols, how we can lay out with them whatever shapes of thought and feeling we experience. The game acts as a reminder that the alphabet—as David Sacks puts it in his book *The Alphabet*—is "a spectacularly successful invention," comparable in its impact on human history to the invention of the wheel.

Given that the set of wooden Scrabble is now more than sixty years old, and that it was taken from my childhood home in Ireland to all the places that I've lived in since, it's still in remarkably good condition. Only one letter is missing. At the end of our game, we realized there was no *K*. It's not alone in being lost. In reading about the history of the game, I came across an interesting piece online that appeared under the auspices of the New England Historical Society. After the serious business of outlining how the game began, with details about Alfred Butts and James Brunot, the article ends with a list of Scrabble Fun Facts. One of these suggests that "there are an estimated one million Scrabble tiles lost in the world— somewhere." Thinking of our missing *K*, and all those other missing pieces, makes me picture them arranged on some gigantic rack in a kind of cosmic Scrabble game, where players have a million letters to choose from, not just seven. And I wonder what stories would emerge if those letters could be arranged to tell how they'd gone astray. Beyond revealing the circumstances of their loss, would they provide sufficient raw material to at least begin to tell the story of our dependence on

the warp and weft of words, the way we use them
to weave the material of the meanings we rely on?

For our game of Scrabble with the old wooden
set, a missing *K* didn't amount to a serious handicap, otherwise we'd have noticed before we fin-
ished playing. But when I realized it wasn't there,
it made me think beyond this single piece; its loss
acted as a prompt to make me try to gauge the impact of a deeper absence. Suppose that instead of
just one letter missing from this particular set of
Scrabble, the whole linguistic contour associated
with *K* was flattened, removed from the catalogue
of speech and writing. How would the landscape
of language—and of perception-understanding—
be affected? Imagine what might be paralyzed if
K's nerve was carefully dissected out of the alphabet's surrounding tissue and completely ex-
punged from the body of our diction.

In his book *The Alphabet*, David Sacks reckons
that in terms of frequency of use, *K* would be the
fourth or fifth least used of our twenty-six letters.
But even with such a relatively unused letter,
much would need to be renamed, recast, reimag-
ined if it disappeared. Think of koalas and kanga-
roos and kingfishers, of karma, kaddish, and the
Kaaba, and don't forget kneading and knitting.
What about krill, the Krebs cycle? What of kisses?
Then there are knots and keys and kidneys. And
that's just to take words where *K* is the initial letter. What of those where it's embedded elsewhere?
What of coke and heckle, stick and cockle? What of
luck and thinking? Which of our ideas, memories,
perceptions include a *K*-shaped element? In our
repertoire of feelings, which ones are tuned to res-
onate at *K*-frequency wavelengths? What objects

in the world generate or echo with this particular symbol and its sound and shape?

When I think of all the Scrabble sets across the globe with missing letters, it nudges into mind a sense of how much there is in the small marks we make on screen and paper, the small sounds that we utter in their register. Our voices are tuned to the alphabet's score; our perception and cognition pour themselves into the shapes of letters, they're geared according to the alphabet's dictation. Whatever ore of consciousness we have has been smelted in language's furnace. The units of our thoughts are sculpted by the moulds of *A* to *Z*. The lost *K* on its own, like any letter, may offer little. But once in its family group, it lets us forge a plenitude of meanings. As Mallarmé put it in his essay "La Musique et les Lettres," letters are "gifted with infinity," and "everything is caught up in their ancient variations."

According to George Steiner, "alone in literature," Franz Kafka "takes possession of a letter of the alphabet; *K* is now his." Perhaps the missing *K* should therefore have reminded me of the arrest and persecution of Joseph K, the tormented protagonist in Kafka's chilling novel *The Trial*. But instead, the letter lost from our old wooden set of Scrabble brought to mind another work of fiction that's also eerily prescient about some aspects of contemporary society. The accidentally missing *K* reminded me of a deliberate and sinister removal, and one applied to much more than just a single letter.

In his famous dystopian novel *Nineteen Eighty-*

Four, George Orwell introduced the concept of "Newspeak." Under the guise of being a modernization, a renovation of language to make it more logical and efficient, Newspeak was in fact designed to limit thought, to ensure that the populace's ideas and feelings ran only in the channels sanctioned by the Party. Newspeak's paring down to a strictly ordered vocabulary and grammar, with all nuance, eccentricity, and ambiguity removed, was intended by the totalitarian regime to make it impossible to express dissent. By stealing away words that would facilitate the expression of individuality, that would make it possible to voice questions, to doubt or to challenge the orthodox position, they intended to enslave the population. Eventually, it would not just become impossible to *express* opposition; people would be rendered incapable even of *thinking* it—because the means to do so, the necessary words and concepts, were being systematically purged from the language. It's a chilling thought. And in the constrained and trivialized diction that's so insistently evidenced across much of our media, it's easy to feel shadows of Orwell's nightmare falling on the real. Though he was writing decades before Orwell, a comment of Charles Darwin's in *The Descent of Man* (1871) flags up precisely the connection between words and thinking that Newspeak seeks to manipulate. According to Darwin, "A long and complex train of thought can no more be carried on without the aid of words, whether spoken or silent, than a long calculation without the use of figures or algebra." If public discourse is pruned to fit into tweets and sound bites, how will we be able to responsibly debate what matters? We don't have to look far to see trains of thought being repeatedly disrupted.

Thinking of how much hinges on what seems so little, of how many doors can be open and shut with the keys of words, and how words in turn depend on letters, I find myself speculating about an addition, something that extends rather than limits, a creative enhancement rather than a censorious curtailment. If, instead of a missing *K*, we invented a new letter, where might it take us? Might it extend the reach of the alphabet, allow us to see and lasso things that had previously eluded us? Would we be able to forge entirely new words, find in the niches of their meaning new ways of saying, of seeing? I like to think of the possibility of Newspeak-in-reverse, a benign version of Orwell's invention, something that vivifies and enriches language, allowing us to express novel ideas, think ourselves into territories previously closed to us. Just as introducing a new color to an artist's palette would create new possibilities, introducing a new letter, and the new words/concepts it could lead to, might have the potential to spark a cognitive revolution.

Of course the idea of a new letter is more a speculative model than a reality—a thought experiment rather than a discoverable entity. I'm not saying such a thing exists, but imagining it offers another way of emphasizing the importance of letters and the words we make from them. And we don't have to invent any fictitious letter to keep our reservoir of words full and healthy and refreshed. There are ways that are real enough by which we can do this. Reading, writing, and talking should be guarantors of linguistic heath. Perhaps my parents were right about Scrabble's educational value; maybe it too helps us to swim against the currents of diminution that threaten to erode our language.

In *A History of Writing* Steven Roger Fischer argues that "letters hold no meaning in themselves." Meaning only emerges when, in combination with other letters, words are made. That may be so, but William Mason is surely right when he says, in *The History of the Art of Writing*, that "there is a whole volume of human history behind each one of the letters." Where did our *K* come from? In origin, it's part of the alphabet that originated in Egypt around 2000 B.C. and came to us by way of Phoenician script. In a Phoenician context it was originally connected to the symbol for an open hand. I was pleased to think of that when I put the old wooden Scrabble game back in its maroon box. I like the resonance that radiates from an open palm. There are elements of greeting, sharing, friendship, and inquiry in that gesture. It's totally unlike a clenched fist's aggressive closure. It points us in the opposite direction to Newspeak; speaks of discovery more than diktat.

Listening to the Music of a Vulture's Egg

Is it more unlikely that the vulture's egg remained unbroken over the fifty-two years it's been in my possession, or that it reached Ireland unscathed after the long journey from wherever it was laid? Both circumstances suggest a history of careful handling. For a long while I kept it with a swan's egg. They sat together side by side on a shelf in a glass-fronted bookcase, each one large enough to fill a gently cupped hand completely, with the fingers only slightly bent. But at some point along the way, probably in the course of one of my many house moves, the swan's egg got smashed. Accidents happen. Birds' eggs are fragile. I find it more remarkable that the vulture's egg has survived intact than that the swan's egg hasn't.

I know where the swan's egg was laid — on the shore of New Lake, near the village of Dunfanaghy in County Donegal, Ireland, on land belonging to my great-uncle's farm. He gave me the egg when I visited as a boy. It was one he'd taken from a nest himself and kept in a down-at-heel cabinet of curiosities whose shabby collection included a tortoise's shell with dried shreds of flesh still attached inside it, a chipped flint arrowhead, a fox's skull missing one incisor, and a fist-sized rock empurpled with a crusting of amethyst crystals.

I don't know where the vulture's egg — a griffon vulture's — was laid, only where I found it

when I was twelve. Improbably, it turned up for
sale in Lisburn, my County Antrim hometown,
only a few miles from Belfast. Griffon vultures,
also known as Eurasian griffons, have a wide
range that takes in southern Europe, North Africa,
and parts of Asia. So the egg might have been laid
in Spain, Morocco, Turkey, Iran, Israel, Kazakh-
stan, India, or even Tibet.

Whoever took the egg must have been determined. Griffon vultures are large enough to be
intimidating. They have a wingspan of between
seven-and-a-half and nine feet, their bodies are
three to four feet long, and they weigh up to twen-
ty-five pounds. With a hooked beak designed for
tearing carrion and a bald-looking head and neck,
the better for reaching into carcasses without getting covered in blood and entrails, they look far
from approachable. They nest in colonies, usually
on cliff ledges, and a pair will defend their precar-
iously sited nest against intruders.

If you want to collect birds' eggs you have to
learn how to "blow" them. It's a simple-enough
process involving the making of small holes at
each end of the egg. Then, as the name suggests,
you apply your lips to one hole and blow—not
too hard, not too gently—so evacuating the per-
ishable contents through the hole at the other
end. The holes my great-uncle made at each end
of the swan's egg were irregular. They looked as
though he might have used a penknife or perhaps
punched them with a nail. However he did it,
the impact caused deltas of tiny cracks to flower
around each uneven puncture, no doubt weaken-

ing the shell. Beside the carefully drilled holes in the griffon vulture's egg, my great-uncle's jagged efforts look inept, the botching of an amateur.

Whether the vulture egg was taken from the nest by the person who so expertly blew it, or acquired by them directly from the nest robber, or through a middleman or chain of intermediaries, I've no way of knowing. But the drilled holes with their perfect symmetry and the absence of any fracture damage, together with the way *griffon vulture* has been printed on the shell, suggests the professionalism of a dedicated egg collector.

I found the griffon vulture's egg for sale, along with scores of other birds' eggs, in a shop that styled itself "antiques and curios" but whose stock suggested "junk." I was twelve years old and a recently reformed egg collector. The shop's eggs might have represented what remained of the original collection the vulture's egg belonged to. Or it could have been that the eggs displayed in the window came from several different collections, a hodgepodge gathered from a range of different sources that ended up in this particular assemblage. Whatever its provenance, the collection the vulture's egg was part of was, when I encountered it, fast disappearing; it was being sold off piecemeal, egg by egg.

I was pleased to buy the griffon vulture's egg together with a few less exotic specimens. They were welcome additions to my own small egg collection, at that point newly stalled. I'd just come to the realization that I no longer felt comfortable about taking eggs from nests. In those days that

was something routinely done by friends and con-
doned by adults, as long as we obeyed the rules:
only one egg to be taken from a clutch, and care
to be exercised so as not to scare the adult birds
and risk their deserting the nest. But what once
seemed acceptable had started to feel wrong. The
aesthetic appeal of eggs remained a potent lure,
but a growing awareness of the life that was quickening inside them made blowing seem too much
like murder. I'd had the unpleasantly awakening
experience of trying to blow an egg that contained
a well-developed embryo. When the egg smashed
with my repeated efforts to evacuate its contents,
it became clear that the on-the-point-of-hatching
chick had been harpooned by the needle that I'd
used to hole the shell. Buying eggs seemed like a
guiltless way of augmenting my collection—acquiring new specimens without getting blood on
my hands.

The griffon vulture's egg was the second largest in the collection. It and all the others were
dwarfed by an ostrich egg. This was the center-
piece of the shop's display and priced accordingly.
It was well beyond what my pocket money could
run to. On several of the larger eggs, the species'
name was written on the shell. The smaller eggs
had tiny numbered labels affixed to them. The cor-
responding names were given on a typewritten list
displayed beside the eggs. The eggs represented
a mix of British and foreign species. All the ones
I recognized were correctly named, so I'd no reason to doubt that the vulture's egg was anything
other than what the writing on it said. Subsequent
checking against pictures and descriptions con-
firmed its identity.

The eggs weren't priced according to any ornithological scale of value. Instead, the shop's proprietor, with a canny eye for what appealed, made the most attractive-looking and the largest eggs the most expensive, with lower prices for the plainer, smaller specimens. If I could have afforded to, I'd have bought them all. The eggs held the appeal of jewels, and seeing them displayed in the shop window, laid out en masse on a large china platter, was like finding a treasure trove. It acted as a magnet for a crowd of boys. We stood at the window after school and on Saturday mornings, our egg lust holding us transfixed by this unexpected, but steadily depleting, bounty. Like me, the others were in part just held in thrall by the raw appeal of what they saw. But they were also calculating what they could afford, matching their modest finances against the prices given on a sheet of paper taped to the inside of the window, and weighing up the pros and cons of any swaps that were proposed.

Buying the eggs singly, or a couple at a time, had a curious feel to it. Yes, there was the satisfaction of acquiring what would otherwise have been unobtainable — the collector's delight at adding new specimens to his hoard. There was an element of competitiveness, too — pleasure in securing eggs that others wanted, and disappointment when they beat me to a prize. But there was also a kind of furtiveness and guilt, a sense that this was something illicit, forbidden. Somewhere in my mind I guess I knew that I was engaged in nest robbing by proxy. Each transaction had the same soiled feel as those occasions when we bought cigarettes in ones and twos from the dingy newsagent's stall in the town's train station.

The fact that I still have the egg, intact, complete, pretty much as I bought it all those years ago, no doubt helps to maintain the luster of my memories. Each time my eye falls on it, or whenever I pick it up, it gives a tangible prompt, recalling the circumstances in which it came into my life. But even if it had been smashed and the fragments thrown away—like the swan's egg—I think this memory would still be a strong one. Even without the egg to prick remembrance with its presence, it feels as if this is something fixed immovably in mind. The picture of that ramshackle antique shop, its beacon of birds' eggs beckoning from the window, drawing a gaggle of boys to stare as helplessly as if they'd been summoned by pheromones, glows in my mind, a little cameo scene, one of those memories that seem permanent. It's like an inner icon whose incandescence burns independently of the egg-ember I still have in hand.

The hoard of birds' eggs is of course the central feature of this icon, its devotional heart. But present in it too is an image of the shop's proprietor: an exotic-looking dark-haired man with a goatee beard, who wore a burgundy velvet jacket and bow tie and smoked thin, pungent-smelling cheroots. He mostly lounged in a battered easy chair at the back of the shop, reading a newspaper and smoking. Customers—or perhaps it was just repeat, small-spending, juvenile customers like me—were given scant attention beyond an unwelcoming scowl and surly service. On the rare occasions when I heard him speak, he did so with a strong foreign accent that I didn't recognize. He caused a certain amount of interest locally in that no one knew where he'd come from, who he was, or how he'd ended up in so unlikely a venture as opening an antique shop in our hard-headed town, where people weren't much given to spending money on things that had no practical use.

How did we know that the proprietor was Russian, and that he'd fled some persecution in his homeland? I'm not sure whether this information came from him directly, or from someone else, or if it was even true. There were certainly some skeptical voices. They claimed to have heard (though the source was never specified) that he was a bankrupt divorcé from Belfast. They dismissed the accent as an affectation. Like the velvet jacket, bow tie, and cheroots, it was designed to create an aura of sophistication. Unsurprisingly, the shop failed to flourish and soon closed. By then, its birds' eggs had all been sold. No one knew what happened to its clutter of old furniture, china, paintings, and tarnished silverware, still less what befell "the Russian," as he was referred to by everyone, whether or not they believed in his foreignness.

The griffon vulture's egg used to be no more than a touchstone of childhood, a token from my personal history that recalls some happy-enough moments from my past. But along the way, something happened to it; it changed. It's no longer just a cozy talisman of memories. Instead, it's now become supercharged with a newfound electricity. Its voltage crackles along previously unsuspected cables to destinations that have nothing to do with childhood. I know the egg is blown; the shell contains nothing within the perfect arc of its empty enclosure. But it's as if the stale, sepulchral space inside it has somehow been ignited, fecundated, vivified with a fire of previously unnoticed connections. When I consider it now, far from appearing as a dusty remnant from a vanished time, an eggshell drilled and blown, defused, long emptied of its charge, it seems to tempt and threaten with the explosive possibility of multiple hatchings.

I'm not sure precisely when or how this happened. It's the result, I think, of a series of accretions that occurred gradually, rather than there being some single moment of dramatic transformation. And there's a strong element of accidentalness about it, too: I might easily never have encountered what has acted on the egg to change it. But because of the course my life has taken since buying it—the people I've met, the books I've read, the places I've visited, the dreams I've dreamt— the mind has forged a ream of links out of the tangle of what came along, cradling the egg in a nest of new associations. It's become less a souvenir from childhood and more a kind of whirlpool that tugs the attention into its currents. Looking at it now, I'm not just taken back to the familiar ground of a Lisburn junk shop in the 1960s. I'm also drawn into far less comfortable territory. The egg hatches images that are more disturbing—more exciting— than anything simple reminiscence could summon. And the new vistas that it shows me are accompanied by something completely unexpected: the strains of flute music, haunting and insistent.

The egg once brought back into mind a catechism of familiar things: the Russian sitting in his easy chair in that dingy Lisburn shop, smoking his strong-smelling cheroots and reluctantly getting up to serve a succession of boys drawn by the egg collection in the window. But now it summons an unsettlingly different set of pictures. I've come to see the Russian not just as the dapper cheroot-smoking figure he used to be, but also as a naked corpse abandoned on a rocky mountainside, his velvet jacket shredded to make a tatter of crude prayer flags. They're staked around him and flutter in the breeze. Vultures congregate beside his body, poised to continue the process they've obviously begun of eviscerating and consuming the cadaver. Far from being merely macabre, an ugly snapshot of physical dissolution effected by the most unsubtle means, my vision of the Russian cascades into a torrent of images. They flow in rich profusion from his embryonic existence, his form moments after conception, through the line of ancestors who kindled it, stretching back—breeding pair by breeding pair—to the moment life began. And braided together with this ribbon of his lineage there's a parallel lifeline. His story has become fused—confused—with that of vultures. I think of the pair that laid the egg, long emptied, that once sat in the window of the Russian's shop and now sits on my bookshelf, a kind of ghost egg, a wraith of absence, the clasped grip of the shell cupped around an emptiness that's somehow become filled with imaginative substance. I picture all the antecedent birds that led to this particular egg, how—pair by pair and egg by egg—they studded time with this life-form's episodic story.

Like the line traced out by the Russian's forebears, the line of vultures leads back, eventually, through a blizzard of different creatures, to the dawn of life's first light, that initial spark that lit the conflagration we're all part of.

From that moment of hard-to-imagine beginning these two filaments of being—two among billions—reach forward, boring their passage through the eons, creating individual after individual until eventually we reach the Russian and my griffon vulture egg and the moments that they occupy. And these moments in their turn are soon left behind as the filaments of species-continuance rush on into the multiple tomorrows they would claim.

Flute music plays and the focus shifts from species history to individual history. I see the Russian moving from fertilized egg to embryo, infant, child, and adult, a tiny fraction of his existence spent as proprietor of a failing antique shop in a Northern Irish town. I see the moment of transaction when I slid the coins, still warm from my pocket, across the counter and he handed me the griffon vulture's egg. Then his life's current crackles forward into regions I can only guess at, until it reaches old age and death. I think of all the griffon vultures alive in the world today, of the corpses they feed on, of the bones now growing in living bodies that will, in time, provide the calcium for eggshells. The slow wave of time's tsunami, surging from beginning to end, is of course impossible to picture. But sometimes it can be fractionally glimpsed in the streams of individual passage that flow within it. The Russian, a griffon vulture, you, me—we all create little rivulets of presence whose glint can catch the eye and reflect back something of the saga that contains us.

Where did this cornucopia of images come from? How is a blown egg, emptied of its contents, able to suggest such a rich kaleidoscope of patterns? And why does the sound of spectral flute music weave through them? It's hard to provide definitive answers, but I can identify one of the sparks that helped to ignite the emptiness within the egg, transforming it from confined space filled only with childhood memories into something gravid with a far higher voltage. The spark came when I was reading Tim Birkhead's *The Most Perfect Thing*, his engaging study of the inside and outside of a bird's egg. I was struck by many of the observations he makes. For instance, talking about the appeal that eggs exert, Birkhead casts light on what so powerfully drew me and those other little boys to gaze longingly at the hoard displayed in the antique shop window:

> There is something sensual about eggs. Of course there is: they are part of sexual reproduction, but birds' eggs have an erotic aura all of their own. Perhaps their wonderful curves trigger deep-rooted visual and tactile sensations.

Certainly the griffon vulture's egg, like all the eggs on that china platter, triggered something deep-rooted, connected not just to aesthetic appreciation but to the nerves that run in those thick, hidden cables that pulse with the body's primal urges.

But what really stopped me in my tracks in Birkhead's book was something he said on page 195: "The egg of a griffon vulture weighs 250g and takes forty-nine days to hatch." It wasn't the weight that was arresting — though it's impressive for a bird's egg — but those forty-nine days between laying and hatching. That number stirred memories, forged a connection, and eventually prompted me to rule a mental line between the egg and one of the volumes on the bookshelves below where it's sitting. The line acted almost like a two-way umbilical cord, allowing ideas to flow between egg and book.

No more than half a griffon vulture's wingspan separates the egg from my copy of the *Bardo Thodol*, more commonly referred to as *The Tibetan Book of the Dead*. In fact, that title is of questionable accuracy. It was chosen by W. Y. Evans-Wentz, the American scholar who brought an awareness of this esoteric text's existence to the West. He was influenced in his choice by *The Egyptian Book of the Dead*, but the similarities between the two works are tenuous and indirect at best. A more apt rendering of the Tibetan text's title would be something like *Liberation Through Listening Whilst in the Bardo State*. The bardo state is the postmortem plane of existence in which, so Tibetan Buddhists believe, the newly dead find themselves for forty-nine days. *The Tibetan Book of the Dead* describes the different stages of experience the psyche will undergo during this period, which is seen as crucially transitional between the end of this life and whatever life or state comes next. The *Bardo Thodol*, in other words, is concerned with what happens between the laying of death's egg and its hatching into our next manifestation after its forty-nine-day incubation period. The text is read to a dying person, and also recited by lamas as a kind of prayer for the departed in the immediate aftermath of their demise. The intention is to provide guidance for the deceased, whose psyche will encounter all manner of visions, alluring and terrifying, during its forty-nine-day sojourn on the bardo plane. But reading this spiritual guide is also intended to alert the grieving living to the nature of their existence and what they too will eventually have to face.

For a twelve-year-old boy growing up in Ulster in 1967, a vulture's egg was something utterly exotic. Like the Russian who sold it to me, it spoke of distant horizons, as-yet-unexplored territories. But despite the vividness with which this alien talisman and its acquisition came to be imprinted on my memory, it was a different sort of foreign egg, a different kind of hatching, that was to have a more profound impact on my life. Only a few years after my purchase from the Russian, Buddhist teaching fell upon my adolescent Presbyterian mind with the force of revelation. No doubt its impact was strengthened by a similar aura of exoticism to that which attended the vulture's egg. My first encounter with Buddhism was mediated via a clutch of books: Paul Reps's *Zen Flesh, Zen Bones,* Edward Conze's *Buddhist Meditation,* various volumes by D. T. Suzuki, and of course *The Tibetan Book of the Dead.* It's tempting to see their laying in my mind as a kind of

cuckoo-like process, with alien interlopers displac-
ing the fledglings of my native religious heritage.
But it felt more like a benign cross-fertilization —
even an unexpected homecoming — than any kind
of predatory colonization.

It's a short step from *The Tibetan Book of the
Dead* to the practice of so-called "sky burial," a traditional means of disposing of the dead in Tibet.
Corpses are left in remote designated locations
in the mountains, there to be consumed by vultures. In part, this procedure is simply practical.
Grave digging is problematic in a region of frozen,
rocky terrain. Likewise, a scarcity of fuel makes
cremation difficult. But in part it also underscores
a theological point. After death, the body is re-
garded merely as an empty shell; its live contents
have been evacuated as completely as if it were
a blown bird's egg. Whatever passes on to a new
rebirth (or to the liberation of enlightenment) has
gone. Attachment to the husk of the remnant left
behind would be utterly misguided. As Heinrich
Harrer puts it in *Seven Years in Tibet,* describing a
sky burial he witnessed, for Tibetans their bodies
after death simply "have no significance."

The thought of a body being ripped asunder
and consumed by vultures may seem horrific.
But as Thom Van Dooren observes (in his book
Vulture), "discomfort about the prospect of being abandoned to vultures after death is cultur-
ally specific." So the Parsees of India and Tibetan
Buddhists are accustomed to the practice and re-
gard it without abhorrence. For them, disposal of
the dead by deliberate exposure to scavengers is

something sanctioned by their religious teachings and with deep roots in their history and culture. To a contemporary Western perspective, though, such a practice would be viewed askance; it would be seen as signifying what Van Dooren calls "a kind of abandonment by the human community, a sign that the deceased is not being cared for properly." Yet such funerary practices may not be as alien to Europe as present-day revulsion would suggest. Archaeological finds in Scotland indicate that a form of sky burial was once practiced there, through the agency of sea eagles rather than vultures.

In *Tomb of the Eagles: A Window on Stone Age Tribal Britain*, John W. Hedges describes the discovery made in Orkney in 1958 of a chambered Neolithic cairn near the cliffs at Isbister. Bleaching and weathering of the human bones it contained suggests the dead were given sky burials, with the bodies left exposed to the elements and to scavengers before being collected for interment in the cairn. Of course, it's impossible to say with any exactitude how these ancient people treated their dead, but Hedges favors the hypothesis that "the dead were exposed on constructed platforms with excarnation being effected by decay, carrion-feeding birds, maggots, and the elements." Certainly, judging from the number of sea eagle remains found in this ossuary alongside its hoard of human bones, it seems likely that these magnificent birds fulfilled an important totemic function. Their likely role in stripping flesh from the bodies of the dead is something James Macdonald Lockhart touches on in his 2016 book *Raptor*. After examining the Tomb of the Eagles at Isbister

and the nearby museum devoted to it, Lockhart
concludes:

> That the sea eagles were involved in
> the excarnation of the human dead is
> almost certain given that the bird is
> such a prodigious carrion feeder.

Discovering the griffon vulture's forty-nine-
day incubation period and making the link between this and *The Tibetan Book of the Dead* has
invested the blown egg that sits on my bookcase
with a new potency. Its evacuated contents have
been replaced with a fecund mix of ideas, as if a
rogue quicksilver yolk of unexpected connections
had been covertly injected into its emptiness. The
egg has taken on a weight and gravity it did not
possess before. It summons into orbit around itself a sense of time that ruptures the little scale
of memory's calibration. Instead of looking back
to the moment when I bought it in 1967 and forward to the present and near future, the egg seen
through a lens ground by ideas about the bardo calls into view a more sweeping timescale. It
makes me think of the beginning and end of an
individual's life, the beginning and end of a species' lineage, the beginning and end of time itself.

And what about the flute music, which has
come to weave its mysterious trajectories of sound
around all my vulture's egg imaginings? Why this
particular instrument and not some other? The
notes, tentative yet insistent, stem from another accidentally encountered splinter of informa-

tion—a splinter that now clings to the egg as if it were a shard of iron filings drawn to a powerful magnet. Unlike the forty-nine-day incubation period, exactly where or when I came across this musical splinter I can't recall, but the facts are easily enough recounted. In 2008, what many view as the oldest musical instrument ever discovered was found by archaeologists. Their find was made at Hohle Fels, a Stone Age cave in southern Germany. The instrument was a flute. Originally thirteen inches long and less than half an inch wide, it has a *V*-shaped mouthpiece and five finger holes. But what stuck most in mind was the material used to make this ancient instrument—the wing bone of a griffon vulture.

Finding out about this forty-thousand-year-old vulture-bone flute means that as well as drawing into orbit around it *The Tibetan Book of the Dead*, sky burial, and an expanded sense of time, the egg on my bookshelf has now acquired another satellite. This one takes the form of the shadowy figures of our ancestors putting bone flutes to their lips and blowing. And I can't help wondering as the breathy notes sound in my imagination—notes threaded with the cry of sea eagles—what our forebears heard in the music of the things around them. Could they detect themes and variations that we've grown deaf to?

Blowing eggs, blowing bone flutes. Our breath warm against these hard artifacts conjured by the intimate, unseen metabolism of vultures. Stilled breath, bodies become cadavers, their meat and matter torn asunder and devoured by Eurasian griffons, their substance built into what, years hence, others may make music from. The cycle of

life and death and the faltering notes of our efforts
to make sense of it. What is the true nature of our
flesh and bone and heartbeat across all the centuries in which there's been a human pulse beating
out the rhythm of our theme tune? Are we kindled
and extinguished, built and broken purely in the
realm of the bodily? Is the drama of our species
performed entirely in the theater of what's corporeal, or are there other parts to it beyond the obvious three-act story line of birth and life and death?
Might it be that we are creatures of flesh and blood
and bardo? Is there in some hidden interstice of
our substance the lilting refrain of a flute, its notes
reaching into aspects of us words can't map? Within the emptiness of hollow bones, is there a trace
of some sound-marrow, some stratum from which
breath might awaken notes that hint at something
beyond the blown eggshell of the corpse?

   The vulture's egg I bought when I was twelve
still sits on my bookshelves. It's like an unexplod-
ed bomb that has somehow acquired the power to
detonate repeatedly. If I look at it now, I know my
attention will trigger an explosion of images and
ideas. If I could defuse it, cut its wires of connection, render it safe, I might be tempted—let it become again just a harmless memento of childhood,
something that takes me back no further than that
Lisburn junk shop and its Russian proprietor. Yet
to geld it thus, even if it was possible, would be
to yield to nostalgia and timidity. No matter how
discordant and disturbing it may be, the music
that the vulture's egg contains is more in tune
with the way things are than the usual registers

by which we measure them. We exist in a world whose lineaments are on a scale that dwarfs the simplicities of memory. The contour lines of the quotidian by which we navigate our days seem like a child's scribbling over altitudes and depths that mock such paltry efforts to contain them. I suspect the uncomfortable truth is that however much we might prefer our own familiar refrains, we cannot really pinpoint our location, or calibrate our journey, or see clearly where and who we are without listening to the notes that issue hauntingly from the unlikely orchestra of my griffon vulture's egg.

Particle Metaphysics

Usually, the things around me are silent, self-contained. They lead to nowhere but themselves, suggest no depth beyond their own substance. They point to nothing beckoning in the far distance, forge no links except for the obvious contiguities with whatever's beside them. For the most part they exist unproblematically, within the boundaries set by routine description. They wear without complaint the labels that ordinary vocabulary bestows. So when I look around the room I see *photographs, books, pieces of driftwood, a Buddha statuette, a bowl of apples, two bottles of wine, a clock, a piece of string.* Every item occupies the term used to name it without any sense of constriction or deception. They're all just there, being what they are, regularly encountered elements of the familiar space I occupy.

It's easy to take this routine categorization—the everyday quietude of things—as normal, the standard measure of our days, the baseline that sets the rules for how we see the world, with everything judged and labelled, settled in its own fixed place with the docile obedience of brute existence. But as I've aged, I've come increasingly to think that I've confused something artificial for the natural state of things. Much of what I take for granted as the norm is in fact manufactured—fabricated—and laid carefully over what underlies it, obscuring as much as naming what is there.

What's accustomed, what we're used to, acts as a soporific. It breeds a kind of existential drowsiness, so that we pass our days giving scant attention to what's real.

But sometimes my outlook changes. The everyday containment of things within the bounds we set is ruptured, the usual descriptions fail; the catechism of labels I rely on to make sense of what's around me rings with a hollow note, names lose their grip. It's often hard to identify the factors that lead to this, or to understand why it happens when it does. In lieu of explanation I fall back on images. It's as if the surfaces of things give way like ice so that I find myself floundering in the depths that were beneath them all the while, but hidden by the thin crust of the familiar. The freeze of the commonplace, in which we're normally held safe, is subject to sudden thaws. These unlock its subjugations. As a result, we sometimes fall through to another realm.

Or, instead of freezing and unfreezing/ice and liquid, I think of the ordinary signature of things as being written in the slow, steady current of low voltage. Its illumination provides the glow of what is recognized. But sometimes there's a surge of power; a different kind of electricity appears. It brings an incandescence that's so bright the spidery handwriting of the quotidian is lost. The lacework of definitions and categories we normally rely on is momentarily eclipsed, obliterated by the glare of this newfound brightness. In its dazzle the ordinary measures that we use to orient ourselves are temporarily blanked out.

To better illustrate the nature of this cognitive change of pace, let me bring things into closer focus with an example. There are all sorts of possibilities here. I think almost all of the particles of our experience have the potential to shape-shift out of the garb of the ordinary in which we clad them, into raiment that dazzles and amazes. I've witnessed such metamorphoses across a wide range of things—pencils, leaves, seashells, fossils, paintings—but the example I want to look at here is a photograph. It's an entirely ordinary one, the kind of photo few people would look at twice. In our image-saturated world we're used to the glance sweeping quickly over a whole array of pictures and rarely being arrested by any of them. Our attention skitters quickly across the visual surfaces we're presented with, taking in a rough semblance of what they show, instantly decoding signs, assigning names, constructing meanings, and then passing on. We're hardly ever stopped in our tracks and made to look beyond the rapidity with which the eye routinely sweeps over the things that surround us.

What's pictured in this particular photograph wouldn't halt anyone's gaze—unless they know the place that's shown and are surprised to find its familiar environs made the subject of attention here. It's a picture of no distinction; it has no artistic merit to recommend it. It shows a quotidian-looking urban view, a street scene in some town or city. There are buildings, roads, pavements, vehicles. For all the evidence of human habitation and activity, no people are visible. Nor is there a single blade of grass or any tree to provide a patch of green. It seems an unlikely opening into any realm except the dull territory of what's depicted. And yet this photo has the power to pull me into a different way of seeing, to fracture my usual scales of time and space, and make me rethink the metrics of causation.

Since I took the photograph, I can give details of when and where it was taken, and why I chose to photograph this particular location. But though such details provide some context, they don't, on their own, account for the transformation of an ordinary scene into a kind of vortex, one with the power to draw me into the unpicturable depths that underlie the drab façade of what's shown. Looking at the predictable, reliably ordinary lineaments of this street, the familiar shapes and shadows, who would guess that they could unravel into isobars that trace out a very different weather to the sunny day that's pictured?

As so often with these radical shifts in outlook, the way in, the tipping point, the impetus—I'm not sure what to call it—seems out of keeping with what it leads to. This illustrates again how the extraordinary haunts the ordinary. It's as if dazzling filaments of gold are interlaced with every leaden thread convention weaves to bind the world with sense and make it fit our purposes. When those threads are seen in a particular light, or tugged in a particular way, an alchemy of change results so that, as in this instance, the contours evident in what's plainly before the eye are realigned and the imagination maps a completely different landscape to the one that can be seen.

The photograph was taken in my County Antrim hometown of Lisburn, Northern Ireland. It's a view of Railway Street, one of Lisburn's main thoroughfares. The vantage point I took it from was the footbridge that crosses the railway lines and gives access to the train station's platforms. The photograph dates from the summer of 2007 and has been displayed on my wall since then, one of several that act as tokens of home and belonging — visual prompts of familiar places to remind me of my roots.

I took a lot of photographs of Lisburn in 2007. That year saw the death of my mother (she'd survived my father by two decades), the selling of the family home where I'd grown up, and the imminent prospect of my regular visits to Ireland coming to an end. I knew that this time when I left I'd not be back again for years, if ever. So I was intent on securing a kind of visual transcript of familiar places, photographs that could act as icons of home when I was far away. This photograph is one such icon. Whenever my eyes fall on it, I'm reminded of past times. The picture is so imbued with memories of childhood that an air of warmth seems to emanate from it. Though invisible to any eye but mine, it possesses a kind of illumination; its little scene is haloed by the glow, at once nostalgic and reassuring, of the history that made me.

Looking at the photograph, I'm tempted by a score of hooks, each one sugared with the bait of memory. Bite on any of them and I'm reeled back through the years. It's hard to convey to anyone not born and brought up in these environs how satisfying the sense of intricate dovetailing is between aspects of my life and the scene that's depicted here. Everyone has places they fit into. Their histories happen somewhere, and wherever those histories unfurl they'll create a pattern that provides a template of familiarity, so that seeing it pictured will bring a click of recognition, the sense of pieces of a jigsaw being snugly locked and linked. I realize, of course, that this may bring a sense of imprisonment, of anger and resentment, of claustrophobia or alienation, of regret, rather than any cozy sense of recollection and belonging. Our home places leave us marked in a whole variety of ways, some of them far from pleasant.

For those who don't know the place, for whom Lisburn's Railway Street isn't crowded with an array of prompts to recollection, the photograph will just seem an anonymous urban view of no particular interest. What to me are personalized particularities will to them appear as the blandest of generalities, unmarked by any of those incisions of individual experience that, from my perspective, leave the place lined and creased and scarred into the features of a familiar face.

When I look at the photograph, I know that the red brick building at bottom left is the Temperance Institute. Its original purpose long left behind, it brings back memories of reluctantly attended ballet classes, of standing shivering with cold alongside two other seven-year-old boys, daunted by being in what was, for us, an alien setting, vastly outnumbered by a swarm of censorious and more confident girls. On the same side of the street was the shop where my first-ever bicycle was purchased, and the newsagent where I spent my weekly pocket money building up a collection of the Ladybird series of nature books. A little farther on is the grocery store where I accompanied my mother and watched as she placed orders for goods to be delivered to our house. The assistant who took the order was Mr. McClatchey. He always smiled at me as he reached for the indelible pencil from behind his ear, wet it between his lips, and wrote down what she asked for in his order book, giving her the carbon copy, which he tore out with a flourish when the order was complete. As he leaned on the wooden counter, I was fascinated by two things and mentally ticked them off, looking for them on each visit: the extreme hairiness of his arms and the purple colour of the licked lead of the indelible pencil.

On the other side of the street was a confectioner-tobacconist's called Coulter's, after the family that owned it. It witnessed that small rite

of passage as I moved from buying sweets to buying cigarettes. I still remember the furtive mix of
guilt and pleasure that accompanied my first so
adult-seeming tobacco purchase. Beside Coulter's
was the barbershop where my brother and I were
regularly taken, emerging into the newly noticed
cold with the feel of stubble prickling our necks.
Moving farther down the street, heading back towards where I took the photograph, there's the
old post office, later library, that's now a youth
club, the church we attended (out of sight because
it's set back from the road), and then the light-blue
building on the opposite corner to the Temperance
Institute—ironic placement—a pub called the
Robin's Nest. There, at that awkward juncture between childhood and adolescence, I went drinking
with my elder brother and was ineptly surprised
by the attention paid to me by a girl who'd always
ignored me in the classroom.

So many of the little staging posts of life are,
for me, arrayed along this ordinary-looking street.
I've listed only a handful of them. To flesh them
out in detail or recall more of them would require
a book-length manuscript. Each association connects with others and, given half a chance, would
build into a network that could catch the story of
my childhood. But my intention here is not to write
a memoir. These autobiographical fragments are
incidental. I'm interested in exploring the way in
which this photograph of a familiar place, heavy
with the cargo of memories it carries, can also
sometimes morph into something else entirely.

What changes, so that instead of acting as an

icon of the familiar, a little cameo holding welcome echoes of home and childhood, the photograph instead becomes something other and unnerving? How did it become an entrance into territory calibrated according to noneveryday parameters, whose scale dwarfs my personal story into insignificance? What unzips the skin of the recognized to leave me floundering in what lies beneath it? It's not always easy to identify the factors that lead to the ordinary particles of experience metamorphosing into something extraordinary and, in the process, causing massive changes in the psyche's inner weather. But in this case, at least part of the cause is clear enough. It stems from the shrapnel that issues from what I think of as a rogue memory. It doesn't come back every time I look at the photograph. But when it does, it temporarily eclipses the routine childhood ones. This rogue memory has a very different reference range to those routine childhood ones of ballet classes, bicycles, grocery store orders, haircuts, cigarettes, and churchgoing.

When I was in my late teens and early twenties, Northern Ireland was in the grip of the Troubles. One day, at their height, I was walking along Railway Street. I'd just passed the Robin's Nest when sirens began to blare and police appeared, urgently moving people away from that end of the street. Along with others, I was marshalled quickly past the church, the old post office, Coulter's — at which point the bomb exploded. Turning at the shocking sound of the blast, I saw smoke and flames billowing out of an insurance agent's office just before the church. I'd walked past it only moments earlier.

Whenever I recall the explosion now, years later, I can't help rewinding that day into different recensions. Then the photograph becomes less a static image of the moment that it pictures, more a kind of kaleidoscopic lens that offers a range of variations on the theme of what happened on that day. Looking at it underscores what's obvious but easily forgotten—namely, how easily circumstances can change, rendering outcomes completely different. If I'd delayed for a few minutes longer to watch the Belfast to Dublin express train speeding through Lisburn station as I crossed the footbridge on my way into town; if I'd stopped to tie a shoelace; if I'd met a friend and we'd chatted for a while; if the traffic had been so arranged that I'd had to wait a few minutes longer to cross the road—if any of the innumerable things that preceded my walking along Railway Street had been altered, even fractionally, I might have been passing the insurance agent's office later than I did and so been caught in the full force of the blast.

Going beyond these obvious proximate causes of alteration or delay, the contingency of what happens becomes ever plainer as the realization gathers pace that changing the texture of events at any juncture of a life could radically transform the way they play out into our futures. How might that point in time have been refashioned if, say, ten years earlier I'd looked a little longer than I did at a view from a mountaintop, or spoken three sentences more (or less) in a long-forgotten conversation, or chosen to go right instead of left at a crossroads on a country road? Looking at how easily things might have been otherwise highlights the way in which events seem dependent on a complex backstory of intricately interwoven causes and effects. Snip one link, retie one knot of circumstance, change a moment's duration, accelerate or slow the tempo of a kiss, a step, and the whole pattern of a life may be scarcely altered, or it may shimmer into an altogether different shape, or simply be snuffed out.

Thinking back in time like this, tracing my footsteps from the moment that I turned and saw the blast, I find myself reaching further and yet further back, imagining the proliferation of events that lock into place through eons of the past before leading to these few moments in the transient reality of their here and now, happening as they did at just this time in just this place. Such imaginings quickly arrive at destinations that long predate all the things I recognize. Before Railway Street was built, before Lisburn was a town, before *Ireland* was a word, before any languages were spoken, before *Homo sapiens* emerged, what was here in this space framed by my photograph? And what will be here a thousand or a million years from now? And how do all of the things that have happened, that are happening, and that will happen here in this familiar/unfamiliar territory relate to each other? What do they mean? Where do they ultimately lead?

I'm used to mapping with coordinates so limited they reach little further than my own fleeting transience. But just beneath the shallows of such measures there are oceanic depths of distance and duration and causation. Any of our timelines can be followed backward—or forward—in this way. They soon vanish from the reach of our individual experience into realms of dwarfing ancientness and futurity. Whoever made and placed the bomb, whoever phoned a warning, the woman led away with blood streaming from her head, everyone in the angry crowd that gathered soon after the detonation, all of them—all of us—are part of a saga that dwarfs the episodic narratives of our brief, single lives. What history maps is but the tiniest, most superficial fragment of what passes. We see no more than a scintilla of what is there.

My photograph of Railway Street in 2007 shows somewhere untroubled. Despite the bomb blast that I witnessed there, the bulk of my memories of the place are tranquil. I remember it with affection as a familiar place of childhood, a scene of scores of those little transactions that, in their unremarkable happening, weave together the fabric of a life. I don't think of it as a place of violence or mayhem. But I realize that the way it seems will depend on the coordinates of time that are selected in which to view it. Go back a century and you could follow the route taken from the house at number 31 Railway Street to the Church of Ireland cathedral, whose narrow spire is visible in the photograph. Oswald Ross Swanzy walked that way to attend morning service on Sunday, August 22, 1920. On his way back, at the corner of Railway Street and Market Square, just outside the Northern Bank, he was assassinated by the IRA, who believed he'd been complicit in the killing of Tomas MacCurtain, Lord Mayor of Cork and a high-ranking IRA leader. The shooting of Swanzy, a district inspector with the Royal Irish Constabulary, sparked the worst sectarian unrest in Lisburn's history. Numerous reprisals were taken on the town's Catholic population, with many properties destroyed and families driven out. I sometimes think of that when I look at the photograph of Railway Street. It acts as another reminder of how this place, like any place, has played host to all sorts of stories. But for me, far from being a way into Ireland's troubled modern history, my icon-photograph of Railway Street alternates between the scales of childhood and those that answer to a vastly more encompassing calibration.

Looked at in one way, the photograph of Railway Street acts as a reassuring touchstone of childhood, a memento that sparks remembrance of a sheaf of ordinary events. Looked at another way — a seismic shift of perspective — it acts as a path that leads out of the known into the vertigo of time and space and possibility that cradles us in the cupped hands of its amplitude. Underlying this familiar street is the same abyss that runs beneath all the moments that we occupy, all the places we traverse. The coordinates of time and place and chance imagined in their entirety, not overwritten with the paltry scribbles of our names and dates and whatever happens to us, makes plain the wild improbability of our being here — the preciousness of life. It's sad that our loyalties so often fix on the blinding immediacies of what's within our reach, to the extent that the unlikeliness that shimmers around every event — the sheer wonder of our existence — gets missed.

I've come to think of there being two ways of reading our experience. We can apply the physics of common sense, what we're used to, corral things securely within the ambit of the everyday, measure them with the calipers of the quotidian. Or we can take a metaphysical perspective, one that looks past the commonplace to the fundamental nature of things, sees how they appear *sub specie aeternitatis*. What I find curious is the way in which some of the particles that we encounter — and for me the photograph of Railway Street is one of them — don't sit securely in either outlook but shift unpredictably between them. These unstable elements can be unsettling, moving in a trice between spending boyhood pocket money on nature books to thinking about deep-time and causation. But rather than insisting on one perspective or the other, I try to welcome both. We humans are, or need to be, cognitive amphibians, equally at home on the dryland of the ordinary and in the water of the extraordinary that laps — enticingly, terrifyingly — around it.

Blood Owls

These are not things you would associate with liquid:
- Perching motionless for hours,
    hidden in a tree
- Flying silent and invisible across
    a field
- Navigating safe passage through
    the dark
- Dropping with lethal precision in
    a calculated pounce
- Coughing up bone and fur-filled
    residue

Yet it is in terms of liquid that I think about them now, the owls that so entranced me all those years ago. Then, although fugitive, rare, elusive, hard to see, they still seemed ordinarily solid. Like hawks, wrens, blackbirds, sparrows, and finches, owls were part of the accustomed birdlife in those few wooded acres of the County Antrim countryside that I spent so much time exploring as a boy.

Of course it would never happen, but supposing an owl let you reach out and grasp it. It would, like any bird, resist the hand with its presence. Instead of encountering no more resistance than a pool of water would create, the grip would close on the body's feathered substance. Its live flesh, muscled beneath the softness, might be startling in terms of the shock of reaching out and finding a wild thing still there, shimmering with vibrancy beneath your fingers. But for all the strangeness of finding it not fled, it would still fall within the repertoire of what's material, concrete, corporeal; it would never be mistaken for the feel of liquid.

What changed, so that in my recollection of them now owls have acquired a fluidity that never struck me then? Can the cumulative weight of passing years act upon a memory so that, eventually, it changes form, turning even the hardest pearl of compacted remembrance back into the water of what passes? Does the freezing of a moment that's saved from the oblivion of forgetting inevitably thaw over time, so that the icescapes of the past melt in our mental grasp, slowly changing shape until they merge with the fathomless waters of what's forgotten, its bleak expanse unmarked by any breath of those mnemonic currents whose ripples prompt the phantasms of recall?

Although the mysterious fluid mechanics of memory no doubt play a part in things, I think this metamorphosis of owls stems mostly from an insight that's grown as I've aged. This recognizes that even the best sightings I had back then were only minutely fractional. Decades separate the writing of these reflections from my boyhood owl watching, but I can remember a few cameo scenes with a vividness that shrinks the years. For instance:

—The moment when an owl flew directly towards where I lay concealed, watching. It came so close that even in the failing light of dusk its eyes seemed to blaze.

—Discovering a roosting owl one summer's afternoon, its presence in a spruce tree betrayed by a scattering of pellets on the ground below. Looking up, the rich colors and intricate patterning of its plumage were set off to perfection against the dark trunk and foliage.

—Climbing to a nest and finding two owlets, strange, otherworldly-looking creatures, gazing back at me.

But despite their lasting impact, I realize now that the nature of these encounters was very different from how I perceived them at the time. What felt like complete experiences, satisfying in their wholeness, were no more than tiny droplets, spray from the huge waves of an ocean I was blind to. It surged its presence through every conduit of circumstance in that place; every moment was tidal in the immensity of what it carried, suffused with a cargo that dwarfed my simple way of seeing. Yet it's only now, in retrospect, that I can sense the water's presence, feel something of its scale and power, hear the roaring of the surf.

Perhaps I needed this space of years to pace through—stepping back and further back—until those days came into proper focus. Maybe up close, in the immediacy of our lived moments as they happen, the voltage of experience is so intense that it demands instant earthing through the vocabulary of the accustomed. Thus we label and name things according to the taming metrics of the mundane. But time's passage has afforded me safe distance. A different picture now explodes out of the constraints of the everyday.

The long-eared owl (*Asio otus*) is very much a creature of the night. That doyen of bird photographers, Eric Hosking, describes them in his autobiography *An Eye for a Bird* as "the most nocturnal of all the British breeding owls." They are superbly adapted for hunting in the dark. Their eyes are rich in cone cells to enhance night vision. According to John Lewis-Stempel (in *The Secret Life of the Owl*), a long-eared owl would be able to see a mouse in a light level equivalent to a single candle burning in an area the size of a football stadium. Their hearing is honed to a similar pitch of sensitivity. Large, asymmetrical ear openings are designed to detect tiny squeaks and rustles and pinpoint their location. The owl's own flight is silenced so that prey will not be warned of its approach, nor will the owl's aural scan be muddied by the sound of its own movement. Feathers are fringed along their leading edges and have a velvety pile on their surface. This mutes the sound made when the bird is moving. If you take an owl's primary wing feather and sweep it vigorously through the air, it makes only the faintest whisper. You have to concentrate to hear it. The feather of a crow or pigeon moved in the same way is raucous by comparison.

Although worldwide it has an extensive breeding range—across much of Europe and many areas in North America and Asia—this is yet an uncommon and secretive species. The RSPB (Royal Society for the Protection of Birds), Britain's leading bird conservation charity, describes long-eared owls as breeding "thinly" across the country and estimates that there are only somewhere in the region of 1,800 to 6,000 pairs. It's not surprising, therefore, that most people have never seen one. This contributed strongly to the allure they held for me. Their rarity enhanced a sense of having glimpsed something special, secret, verging on the sacred, on those rare occasions when I had the good fortune to spot one. Seeing a sparrow was commonplace. For an adolescent boy fired with a fierce nature-mysticism and thirsty for wild traces of the numinous, seeing an owl was akin to the revelation of a grail. But what I didn't realize then was that even in the most hallowed moments of encounter I was only seeing a fraction of what was there. The categories by which I understood the world sold it short. They bought into a kind of cognitive bankruptcy underwritten by the base metal of the commonplace rather than the gold of wonder. It has taken me years to see how the economy of the everyday, by which we measure the bulk of our experience, is calibrated according to a scale that's sized to miss much more than it catches.

I'm not saying that I see the whole picture now—no one can do that—but I think I see significantly more of it than I did back then, or at least recognize, as I didn't when I was a boy, how partial our experiences are, even when they strike us as compellingly complete.

Describing something is never easy. That's not surprising given how words fit—don't fit—the world. What we experience can be conveyed but never completely captured on the page. Sentences hint, suggest, point at things, drape their verbal overlay across the landscapes that we want to talk about. Words are designed to represent, not reproduce. If they're well cast, they can nudge other minds into the same broad currents of feeling and cognition that move the writer. But the flow of subjectivity remains inviolably private; we each navigate our own individual life-streams, and no one else can know as we do the weather of our waters, its intimate array of flavors. Writing lets us craft approximations, often to a high degree of likeness, but it can't conjure the perfect echo of fac-simile. Words are for mapmaking, not replicating the territories they're concerned with.

The descriptions of owls I like best aren't the ones that attempt a visual transcription — the sort that try to re-create the bird in words, with details of size, shape, and color given in order to aid iden-tification. I prefer those that take a less literal ap-proach. For instance, "an owl is a cat with wings" (John Sparks & Tony Soper, *Owls: Their Natural and Unnatural History*). Or, looking at owl pellets rath-er than the birds themselves, John Lewis-Stem-pel's picture of them as "little cabinets of maca-bre curiosities." But owls as liquid? That doesn't sound promising at all. How can such an unlikely linkage convey anything except the oddness — the inappropriateness — of the parallel it's suggesting?

The liquid view of owls I've come to have might be described as "haemocentric," given how much it focuses on the lifeblood that they carry. Of course thinking of owls "carrying" their own lifeblood risks creating an erroneous picture. Far from being some kind of cargo that they bear, blood is an intimately integral part of them. It's not as if they load and store it in some hold that's separate from themselves, then batten down the hatches so that it can be safely transported from A to B. Blood rather facilitates their entire alphabet of

movement. Its percolation through the labyrinth
of arteries and veins, the network of capillaries
that riddles every tissue, is what fires the metabolism with the oxygen it needs. In addition, blood
carries nutrients and chemical messengers around
the cells, transports waste, drives and shunts and
filters its cocktails of exquisitely balanced com-
pounds through every region of the bird's corporeality. Kept moving at exactly the right pace by
the heart's pumping metronome, blood bathes the
flesh, soaks through it, seeps into every muscled
nook, warms with its flow the entire territory of
the feather-clad body. Blood and owl are closely interwoven. It's not a case of one carrying the
other; one *is* the other. Blood is a constituent not
a cargo.

This close entwinement of bird and blood not-
withstanding, my liquid view of owls highlights
blood and imagines it as something more than
whatever happens to fill the arteries and veins of
any one particular bird. How many fluid ounces
of blood does a single long-eared owl contain?
How many gallons would there be, supposing every owl in Ireland, Britain, Europe, the world was
drained into a common reservoir? How much owl
blood has there been in the history of this species
taken in its entirety, from the first appearance of
Asio otus millions of years ago to whatever point
in time will see the final faltering heartbeat of its
last surviving representative? It would, no doubt,
be possible to estimate plausible answers to these
questions. But I ask them not so much to spark a
set of sums, calculate amounts, as to shift attention from the usual way of seeing owls—the way I
used to see them—to the way I see them now.

When did owls begin? When did their blood start to flow? It's not yet possible—it may never be possible—to plot the precise coordinates for the point of genesis that saw *Asio otus*'s first appearance in the world, or to trace out the course these creatures have followed in the years since then. Yes, we can assess with some accuracy their current global distribution, compare population densities at different sites, but the long history behind the present situation becomes progressively uncertain the further back we go, though analysis of mitochondrial DNA may hold the promise of unravelling things in more detail. The oldest owl fossils yet discovered date from nearly sixty million years ago. But paleo-ornithology is fraught with difficulties. Being thin and hollow, bird bones are fragile and easily destroyed. Accordingly, the avian fossil record is slight, uncertain, incomplete. Fossils of birds are scarce, hard to identify, and harder to read into the specifics of particular species.

But even if we can't fully map the emergence and evolution of owls as a family, still less pick out the genealogies of the different species, we know enough to recognize that this is a long-established life-form. Each owl I saw in those few wooded acres of the County Antrim countryside was an instantiation of something ancient, an individual reiteration of a body-plan whose blueprint was drawn up eons before that brief moment of encounter. Each owl I saw represented the tip of a living thread embroidered into time. Bird after bird after bird after bird were the needles that pulled it forward, snaking through the centuries, passing owl from body to body as if a feathered

bucket-chain had formed to carry this precise for-
mula of life from its source to its conclusion.

I've come to think of owls as something liquid
because a flow traces more accurately the shape
of what they are than anything that's fixed and
static. To see a long-eared owl gliding towards
me in the dusk is to witness an airborne droplet
of the ancient sea of owl, a fragment of a flying
wave moving to tidal rhythms formed in another
era and incised upon this transient feathered form.
Each cupped receptacle of bird carries forward for
the briefness of its life its tiny share of an astonishing ocean. The flow of blood that laps and ripples
around the little coves and inlets of any single owl
is part of something so much vaster. Owls function much like irrigation systems: their arrangements of organic channels, dams, and sluice gates
are built to hold, carry, and pass on the blood of
what they are, corralling and communicating the
essential life-water of their species, safely conveying it through time.

Locked into the labyrinth of life that we've
named "long-eared owl" a liquid symphony is
playing. Its notes have sounded out for longer than
our species has been around to listen to it. Through
a maze of arteries and veins that stretch their networks across millions of years, the intricate tube-
work laid down upon the stepping stones of individuals, a kind of seriatim seabed, the life-flow
of this species surges forward. It is in liquid that
procreation happens. The eggs, white orbs in the
untidy platform of the nest, are like elevated, independent rock pools, seemingly cut off from the
tide that created them. They hold safe a portion of
enchanted, life-filled water. Until new bodies gel,

their hard shells enclose the brine that's charged with the electricity whose voltage makes an owl. Distilled into the yolk and white is the seed that grows a bird. The bone and flesh and feather that emerge are like flexible eggshell, living porcelain that serves to dam and channel and transmit the vital fluid of *Asio otus*.

Liquid is hard to get hold of; it flows away. Cup your hands and you may catch some for a moment, but it soon escapes. This characteristic fits my new way of seeing owls. The interplay that weaves each individual from, connects it to, the species saga, the way each momentary sighting bears witness to a storyline of eons, the complexity of microscopic processes unfolding in exquisite balance behind the blindfold of the feathers, the ancientness of brain and nerve and pumping heart—such a picture behaves like quicksilver, there for a moment of realization in the mind's eye, then gone again. But it leaves behind, gleaming like a rivulet, the awareness that owl blood has flowed for stellar distances when each circuit around every bird is measured, mile after mile contained within the intimate architecture of the numerous bodies that constitute a kind of living odometer for *Asio otus*. Somewhere in the world right now, this moment, as your eyes touch this sentence, owl blood is being pumped around the network of thousands of owl bodies, as it has been pumped for centuries and will be for centuries to come. Each drop echoes to the throb and thrum of larger processes, an airborne ocean; waves that sit in trees; lethal tsunamis that fall out of the dark, engulfing and absorbing the pooled bodies of their prey.

It's easier with words to focus on static singularities and give the kind of descriptions that a field guide would, focusing on plumage, habitat, behaviour, noting the size and color of the eggs, incubation time, and such like details. It's much harder to capture owls' real dimensions. How could a sentence hold something of this scale and intricacy? How could words be cast so that they convey what lies beyond the simple immediacies of perception? And yet words are not as helpless for giving a liquid view of owls as they might at first appear. Thinking of the way the pen I use touches the page and draws the ink out into the shape of my sentences, there's an unexpected parallel with owls. Just as I'm tapping into the reservoir of language for a clutch of words to contain my meanings, so the individual birds function like owl-pens, drawing out the bead of their existence across the pages of being, channelling from the reservoir of owl the trickle that they need to power their single lives. Each life holds in suspension for its short span a segment of an ancient bloodline, provides a stretch of living piping that allows it to flow incrementally forward, life by life, via the stepping stones of individuals, into unfurling time. As meaning flows through the careful irrigation systems we build with sentences upon a page, so the life-liquid of owls flows, controlled and channelled and contained, through the domain of every bird.

A treasured relic from my owl-watching boyhood sits on the desk beside me as I write this essay. It's a long-eared owl's skull. I took it from a bird that I found shot, its bloodied body lying with a dozen or so crows and a scattering of pigeons

and smaller birds. Men from a village near one of
the woods where I watched owls sometimes came
out after dark with pump-action shotguns and
fired round after round into the trees where they
thought the crows—which they considered ver-
min—were roosting. Their indiscriminate shooting caught any species that happened to be in the
same vicinity. The owl was badly damaged. I kept
some feathers for a while and carefully cleaned the
skull. It's paper-thin, almost translucent, like the
finest bone china. Looking at the huge eye sockets
I can picture the orange-rimmed eyes that used to
fill them. Touching the hooked beak, the tip still
sharp, there's an echo of the violence hard-wired
into this remnant. But what strikes me most is an
imagined sound. The skull is like a kind of seashell
found in my beachcombing of that wood's leaf-lit-
tered strand. Without even having to lift it to my
ear, I can hear the sea in its little echo chamber—
not the Atlantic or Pacific but the Ocean of the
Owl, the wash of blood, synovial fluid, humours of
the eye, saliva, digestive juices, sperm, hormones,
mucous. Sometimes I think this empty skull contains an invisible whirlpool. The bone that dams
and contains it is perilously thin, porous, liable to
fracture. This has led to a kind of corrosive—but
I hope creative—leakage that erodes old certain-
ties, old ways of seeing. The truth is that my liquid
view of owls has seeped into my imagination. I
can feel it changing the way I think about a whole
ream of other creatures, myself included.

Pulse

How could you describe this heart in words
without filling a whole book?

—Leonardo da Vinci*

*Written next to his drawing of the heart and its blood
vessels (c. 1513), held in the Biblioteca Ambrosiana, Milan

Three hearts in a line
Systole, diastole
A moment passes

Would a creature with hearing a thousand times more sensitive than mine recognize the moment by its signature of heartbeats?

Such an exquisitely attuned auditory sense might be overwhelmed by the crudities of engine noise, voices, tires making contact with the road, the shush and rustle of leaves as the wind gusts through them—all the cacophony of sound within which the three that interest me are embedded. Nonetheless, I like to imagine some huge-eared bat or unlikely lizard that's able to filter out all of these distractions, a fantastic beast that could fix in the radar of its hyperaudition the moment I want to examine. Angling its head to precisely the right tilt, it picks out a single aural thread—the pulse of three hearts beating momentarily in sync.

Listen.

Three systolic contractions squeeze together, each pushing through networks of soft, receptive tube-work the gush of blood on whose tidal surges bodies depend.

This is a moment when, if a vertical line had been drawn from the surface of the water to four meters above the roof of the bus in which I was travelling, it would, for a split second, have passed through the muscled chambers of three hearts as they pumped the lifeblood around the bodies in which each of them was snugly enfolded. At the coordinates linked by this imaginary line, the familiar note of my own pulse was joined by two smaller, faster-beating hearts held suspended in the air, one directly below mine, one directly above it: a trio of hearts accidentally aligned, skewered together invisibly on the isobar of simultaneity that ran like a quicksilver filament through a few seconds of the morning.

Or, more prosaically:

Ten minutes into its journey, the bus I take to work crosses a bridge over a river. The nearby estuary attracts a range of wading birds. One morning an oystercatcher was flying close to the surface of the water, following the river's course as it flowed seawards. The bird vanished under the bridge just as the bus crossed it. I imagined the oystercatcher's streamlined body, like a little beacon, briefly illuminating the dark beneath the bridge with the tracer glint of its red eye and orange beak. At exactly the same moment, a curlew — disturbed from its foraging in a roadside field — flew overhead, also in the direction of the estuary. The speed and angle of both birds' flight paths coincided with the bus's progress so that at one point, for an instant, the curlew was directly above me, the oystercatcher directly below, our three hearts thudding out their rhythms.

It's easy to assume that this prosaic description gives a reliable account of the moment, that the raw innocence of its accuracy paints a truthful picture. But in fact this kind of supposedly literal account isn't that at all. Far from being a transcription of what happened, it's a kind of blindfold — woven of convention, attenuation, simplification — by which the nature of things is obscured. The picture I've just fixed upon the page masks rather than reveals; it deceives as much as it describes.

In order to better grasp the moment, to get a sense of the rare particularities of its texture, imagine the oystercatcher and curlew marking the sky with visible traces of their presence, leaving behind miniature contrails, scaled-down versions of those signature lines of condensed vapor that are written by jet aircraft as they crisscross the blue above us.

Let's take the oystercatcher as example and pace our way along its contrail—the line that plots the route it followed to the moment when it flew under the bridge. Like a film played in reverse and speeded up, it's possible to imagine the oystercatcher being retracted along the full length of its lifespan, moving against the current of the tributary down which it has progressed.

Like all its kind, this oystercatcher is a handsome bird, striking in its livery of black and white. The plumage is complemented by a long orange beak, pink legs, and eyes that have red irises. The eyes are rimmed within an encircling orange line that's the same hue as the beak. The pupil is black, and this dark center of the eye acts to emphasize the color around it. The bird's piping call, often made while flying, has about it both an urgency and soulfulness that make it memorable.

As it's pulled back along the contrail of its history, the spoor of its presence in the world, there will be a variety of bursts of flight, landings, take-offs. The oystercatcher will pace and feed on mudflats, sandy beaches, fields. There will be moments of danger as a fox or peregrine threatens. The bird will peck and fly and roost, display and preen and molt. It will experience the passing of the seasons.

In their nine-hundred-page monograph *The Avian Egg*, an attempt "to compile all the facts known about the bird's egg," Alexis and Anastasia Romanoff start by quoting a remark of nineteenth-century ornithologist T. W. Higginson: "If required on pain of death to name instantly the most perfect thing in the universe, I should risk my fate on a bird's egg." Eventually, if we wade back up the contrail-tributary of the oystercatcher's life, we will reach its source in the perfection of an egg.

The oystercatcher that flew under the bridge will have begun its life safely encased in the cupped containment of a well-camouflaged egg, laid with a clutch of others in a rudimentary nest that's not much more than a shallow scrape in the ground. The eggs are streaked and splotched with brown and black on a background that varies in tone from understated yellow to buff or sepia. Their color and pattern mean that the eggs blend perfectly with the earth and stones around them. Warmed by the parents' body heat, incubation lasts for three or four weeks. The chicks that hatch are as well camouflaged as the eggs. It takes a month before they can fly, three years before they're ready to breed.

I'm struck by one detail at the beginning of an oystercatcher's life: "Before hatching, the chick starts to call in the egg and the brooding parent converses with it and its siblings by means of soft cries." It's as if the chicks are using sonar to test for depths beyond the shell, and that the parents, hearing it, summon their offspring, reaching out with song—a tuneful beckoning to break out of their confinement.

Having traced its contrail back from bridge to nest, and to this moment of summoning and being summoned from the egg, it's easy for the imagination to turn things round again and picture the ordinary gravity of time's progression restored, so that it draws the oystercatcher from its egg through all the instances of its life until the moment when its heart beat directly under mine—and to imagine it flying on from that accidental intersection of lives to whatever lies in store for it.

Following the contrail like this is a beginning. It points a way out of the cozy shallows of a "literal" account. Perhaps such contrail-following could be likened to drilling a little way into the rock of the commonplace so that explosives may be inserted. To explode the limiting terms of ordinary description requires the laying of four charges, the lighting of four fuses — a quartet of detonations to shatter the opacities that normally constrain our vision.

First, we need to remember that our unaided senses reveal only a minuscule fraction of the world. Consider what a wealth of things is cloaked by feathers and by flesh, what intricacies our sight is blind to, how much is held invisibly within the forms that capture our attention.

Take an oystercatcher's heart. About the size of a walnut, it would fit neatly in the palm. Held there, it would be more likely to occasion revulsion than wonder; it would appear as a warm, wet nugget of meat, antlered with the aorta's tube-work. But examine it more closely and what meets the eye initially as just a bloody piece of flesh resolves itself into an exquisitely formed organic pump that's breathtaking in the perfection of its design. Unseen, it powers the flow of blood around a network of living channels that branch and spindle their way through all the secret territories of the body, gently fingering into every interstice of its substance. In their varying bore — the relatively massive diameter of the aorta and pulmonary vein, the hairline apertures of the smallest capillaries — the blood vessels are like organ pipes through which the heart plays this bird's life-music.

Scanning electron micrographs reveal astonishing detail about how the intricate sculpting of the heart is fashioned, laying bare the plans according to whose bio-blueprints the bird's foundations are laid down and built on with an array of interlinked structures. But fantastic though these inner nano-landscapes are, they hide yet further secrets whose existence the unaided eye could never guess at and that our other senses are likewise not calibrated to catch. Magnify and magnify again, subject the oystercatcher's heart to the minutest scrutiny, and we'll eventually arrive at the atoms that undergird things with their improbable interplay of particles, their nuclei of protons and neutrons, each in turn laden with the quarks that make them, the electrons orbiting around them in the hard-to-envisage spaces stretched out deep at the core of things. As it flew beneath the bridge, trillions of electrons were following their orbital paths around the atomic nuclei set deep within the hidden groundwork of the oystercatcher's fabric. It's as if there are numerous little planetary systems secreted in the hidden heart of matter, where particles, like stars, follow their celestial trajectories in miniature.

The second charge to lay, the second fuse to light, involves remembering that the oystercatcher's contrail is not the only one. To paint a fuller picture would necessitate following the curlew's contrail too, and mine, mapping out the courses we each have followed. Like the oystercatcher's, the curlew's contrail would lead back to a source in nest and egg, whilst mine would lead back to the embryo I once was, nestled in the fastness of my mother's womb. In order to arrive together at that moment on the bridge, arrayed for a few seconds one above the other, think of all the channels through which our lives had to percolate, the tracks we had to follow, the maze-ways of particularity that were paced out, the weight of history that was distilled to issue in the unique happenstance of presence and passing as three heartbeats pulsed in sync.

This second charge aims its shockwaves at our tendency to focus on things singly. Alongside the oystercatcher's, there are other contrails and each of them bears within it the same wealth of detail. Both for me and for the curlew, and for the other passengers on the bus, the roadside trees and grass, all the visible forms that meet the eye in its immediate unaided scan, what we see is only a fraction of what's there. Beneath the masking integuments of surface plumage, under bark, beneath the skin, there lie the same symphonic complexities of history and substance. Installed in intricate detail within each iota of existence is architecture at which to wonder. Our ordinary perception is geared to noticing very little of it.

The third explosive charge that can help free the moment from confinement in our usual terminology is one that directs attention to beginnings.

Whatever obvious themes and variations we can
identify when we watch the bird, the music that's
centered in an oystercatcher's heart starts sotto
voce, its first trills sounding in the egg. And those
first few notes point to questions that litter life's
threshold. When does the heart's music start?
Where did the beat of this bird's life-rhythm begin? Such interrogations hint at an acreage of notes
massed behind the simple singing that any single
bird can summon.

Initial cardiac contractions can be detected only
thirty-five hours after incubation of the egg begins. Before the harmony of circulation settles into
the rhythms that will animate the bird throughout
its life, there's the incredible introit of embryonic
development. This involves a cascade of interlocking processes, waves of change that surge through
the egg, their tides pulling into shape the life-sand
of the chick. The heart is formed out of the primary and secondary heart-fields — territories of
cells that develop soon after fertilization and that
are somehow imbued with heart potential. Hard-
wired into them, like dance moves in a clockwork
marionette, are the crucial opening bars of the oystercatcher's music. The steps taken by these cells
as they migrate according to the patterns that will
weave the adult bird together, take them through
phases of flexion, torsion, displacement, and re-
absorption that have been rehearsed and refined
over millennia. Miniature ridges, grooves, folds,
and loops emerge and disappear as new flesh is
sculpted into form. A septum appears, a flange
develops, cusps and valves thicken and stretch
as the simple cardiac tube that is the emergent
heart's first shape is transformed into a sophisti-

cated four-chambered pump that's able to power flight—"the most strenuous activity in which any vertebrate engages." The processes of embryological development are conducted in perfect time with one another, their orchestration minutely coordinated as they engineer a heart (and lungs, brain, eyes, kidneys, liver). This is how the heart that beat under mine that morning on the bridge began, this is how it first took form; this is part of the texture of its rhythm. Each contraction echoes with this backstory.

I'm much taken by the fact that the size of an oystercatcher's heart "increases by more than a thousand times during the embryonic period." This happens in a beautifully controlled proliferation of cells into their deftly interconnected and differentiated roles and structures, all kept intimately in tune with each other as they align themselves into the necessary patterns. As the adult birds sit incubating the eggs, these microscopic processes are roiling beneath them. It's as if the eggs each contain a kind of life-storm, a hurricane of controlled energies raging within the calm containment of the shell.

Of course this third charge—the fuse lit by embryological development—burns in the other contrails too. Follow the curlew's or mine back to their source and similar processes of cellular differentiation will have happened. There will be differences naturally, but each of the three heartbeats began with intricate processes of budding and building as fertilized eggs built their life substances into shape. The moment on the bridge has these developmental whorls marked indelibly in the fingerprints it leaves. And were we to examine any of

them minutely, we would again move eventually
from the ballet of cells — from the processes that,
as Gavin Francis nicely puts it, "perform the silent
industry of life at the microscopic level" — to the
nano-world of atomic particles. The wheeling of
electrons around nuclei happens within the egg,
within every aspect of the embryo, within each
cell.

The fourth charge is the largest. Its blast breaks
through to breathtaking vistas. So far, my cartography of the moment has highlighted three individual heartbeats. In considering the complex
microscopic worlds that each heart harbors in its
deep structure, in looking at the processes of embryological development, and in keeping in mind
the fact that the rich complications uncovered by
my focus on the oystercatcher also occur in other
contrails, the emphasis throughout has been on
beings that can be identified, pointed to, named.
But all the close scrutiny so far undertaken leads
only to the false summits of individual beginnings. Again taking the oystercatcher as example,
let me show how the dendrites that form the nerve
of the heartbeat moment on the bridge are rooted
far more deeply in time than in the shallow soil of
single lifespans.

It's easy to make the mistake of supposing that
the oystercatcher's story begins in the egg. If we
trace its contrail back from the moment that the
bird flew under the bridge, there's a strong sense
of reaching the source when we arrive at the nest,
cupping in its shallow hollow a clutch of eggs,
each one primed and brimmed with life. It's surely

from here that the filament of the oystercatcher's lifeline starts the unspooling that will take it to the moment when, for an instant, its heart beat under mine. An egg's clearly defined containment, the sleek lines of its globular solidity, makes it seem a plausible point of origin. But in fact it represents the continuation of an already ancient story rather than any virginal beginning. It may indicate the start of a new individual episode, but it's an episode that's part of an ongoing saga.

Listen to the oystercatcher's heart, but *listen!* Imagine my hyperauditory creature with its supersense magnified another million times. It will be able to hear not just the individual beat of this one bird's heart, quickening as it flies, but the whole history that's engraved into the little two-stroke engine of its repeated systole and diastole. The story of its origin and development across millennia is wound like filigree into every beat. Isolating the oystercatcher's heartbeat from mine and the curlew's, and from all the sounds in which these three are embedded, my hyperauditory creature could savor this pulse—not as a solitary heartbeat but as a long thread of sound stretching back through all the generations on whose existence "my" oystercatcher depends for its own few moments of existence.

The heartbeat under the bridge, like every heartbeat, reverberates not only with its own soft thud, sounded within the muffling chamber of one body; it also echoes with the story that has forged it. The little sluice and wash of liquid pumped around an oystercatcher's body are deceptive. The heart and its network of arteries and veins contain no more than a glass or two of blood. But swarmed invisibly behind them is the reservoir from whose depths they pull the succor that sustains them. The blood that courses around the shape that we name "oystercatcher" is ancient; it took millions of years to distill it. It has been flowing now for eons. The little fluxes created by this one bird's beating heart point to more massive tides and currents. Although its accumulated lifeblood would scarcely fill my cupped hands, each droplet resonates with an oceanic tonnage.

Think of all the hearts before it without whose beating this heart would never have quickened into life. Recognizing the presence of these precursors, the heart that beat under mine that morning seems like the uppermost card in a thick pulsating deck. Cut the deck anywhere, turn the card over, and there's another oystercatcher pictured. Cut again and another one appears, each with its heart pumping around its body a few milliliters of lifeblood. Or, more accurately, look at the card immediately below my oystercatcher and there are two birds. The cards beneath each of them will show in turn two more. Underlying every individual bird are two parent oystercatchers. The deck is thousands of generations deep as, two by two, the oystercatcher bloodline stretches back. The contrail of the bird that flew along the river and underneath the bridge just as my bus was crossing it doesn't just lead back to a neat beginning in an egg.

How far back does this contrail stretch? According to Gareth Dyke and Gary Kaiser in *Living Dinosaurs*, their study of the evolutionary history of birds, primitive versions of the birds we see today "appear in the Early Cretaceous, 120-million years ago." But it's not as if the contrail stops there. Before those primitive versions there were other

life-forms that led to them; before them others yet
again. The contrail pushes back and further back,
like a capillary running deep into the flesh of time.
Like all bloodlines, the oystercatcher's is rooted in
the first glimmers of life on this planet. This is the
pace and tempo at which an oystercatcher's heart
is set. Cargoed in the pulse beneath the bridge,
that momentary muscular contraction, is the saga
of the species; storied into each percussive beat
is the call-sign of the race. Eavesdropping on the
moment, my hyperauditory creature would surely
hear the pulse of *archaeopteryx*, the whisper of orbiting electrons.

In following contrails back beyond the false
summits of individual beginnings, what goes for
the oystercatcher goes for the curlew too, and me.
We could trace each one in similar detail, both in
terms of a single body's story and in terms of what
lies stacked behind it, quickly passing from em-
bryology into genealogy, from genealogy into pa-
leontology, from the present into the distant past
out of which it fountains. In my own pulse — evident to the million-times-augmented hearing of
my hyperauditory creature — there is the vestigial
murmur of all the early hominids who came before *Homo sapiens*, if not the whispered thud that
beat in the breasts of those shadowy mammalian
precursors who began to flourish after the great
hearts of the dinosaurs fell silent. Our hearts,
however much they might seem restricted to the
little intimacy of one transient body, beat with a
rhythm that summons crowds and that sounds
through centuries.

In a letter to his grandson Julian, dated March 24, 1892, Thomas Henry Huxley noted that "there are some people who see a great deal and others who see very little in the same things." Our vision of the world can be expansive, encompassing, inquiring, wondering — or narrow, exclusive, unquestioning, exploitative. We can drift through life on the autopilot of convention, or be alert to the nature of what confronts us. Where we set the index of our outlook is in part innate, in part something we learn. But however it's determined, how we see a moment will do much to mold our reading of the world, our valuation of experience. It therefore seems a matter of concern that the nature of the ordinary, the time that constitutes our lives, is so often glossed over with the broad brush of "literal" depictions.

Of course the vertical line I've imagined linking the oystercatcher's heart, mine, and the curlew's is merely a fragment, artificially curtailed. It could be extended from the oystercatcher down into the river and through the mud and rock beneath it. The same continuance could be drawn from the curlew upwards, taking the line farther into the sky and on into space. And on that perhaps endlessly continued line, the isobar of simultaneity drawn out to its full unfathomable extent, a kind of universal nerve, who knows what other hearts might be skewered upon its amplitude? Maybe below the oystercatcher there was a brown trout swimming under the bridge the second that the bus crossed over it. And below the trout again, buried in the mud, there may have been mollusks and worms, their rudimentary organs likewise pulsing with the rhythms needed to sustain them. The line could be ruled right through Planet Earth until it breaks out on the other side of the globe. Then, like the line above the curlew, it could be drawn on into the sky and the boundlessness of space. What other lives might be transfixed by such a line—a swift's, a soaring buzzard's, a flying insect's, passengers' on a plane going over at just that moment? And beyond that there is the possibility of other worlds and other lives not yet discovered.

Thinking about an isobar of simultaneity drawn through the moment on the bridge, using the three hearts as points against which to place an imaginary ruler so that a vertical line may be plotted and continued (endlessly?) in both directions, I'm reminded of an observation of Einstein's: "We have to bear in mind that all our propositions involving time are always propositions about simultaneous events." In the same pinch of time, if we stop to examine it, such events tread heavily upon every second; a sense of spiraling inclusion yawns open in a heartbeat.

The comparatively simple image of a single vertical line, even when it's extended indefinitely in both directions, is only one of the vectors that might be considered. Through any of my triad of hearts a line could be ruled at any angle. The full cargo of the moment is not merely what happens on one tiny fragment of one line, but on every line, ruled at every angle, and continued indefinitely in both directions.

The duration of what falls immediately upon our senses may be short-lived: the oystercatcher and curlew soon fly on, the bus continues on its route, my attention is claimed by other things. But when we stop to think of what a heartbeat is, of why it's there, of where it came from, of how we can describe it, the simplicity of perception is transformed. It's as if a tiny feather, floating down and landing on the ground in front of us, were to take on the weight of mountains when we try to lift it up. As John Muir famously put it, "When we try to pick out anything by itself, we find it hitched to everything else in the universe."

We are very far removed from the sensibility of the hyperauditory creature I've imagined, but even with our blunt capacities we can surely hear traces of another note sounding through the quotidian hum of things. In a celebrated passage in *Middlemarch,* George Eliot speculated about what it might be like if we could hear grass grow and the beat of squirrels' hearts. Such heightened perception might, she warned, be more than we could bear, "and we should die of that roar which lies on the other side of silence." But is it really less perilous to pitch and mute our listening so that we are deaf to the roar that is contained in every moment?

Is the oystercatcher's heart still beating now? There's a strong likelihood that it is, for they're a long-lived species and they flourish in this part of the country. Perhaps, as you read these words, my oystercatcher is piping a summons to its chicks, having heard the cheeps of the next generation issuing from a clutch of eggs cupped in a shallow depression in the ground. Or maybe as I sit at my desk, my heart beating within me, the oyster-catcher will fly over the house, heading again for the river, the bridge, the estuary. Then, for another instant, our hearts will be aligned again, with who knows what co-inhabitants arrayed on the new isobar of simultaneity that could be plotted through the pulse of this – as of every – moment.

Three hearts in a line
Systole, diastole
A moment passes

In the Stomach of a Termite

I'm in familiar territory, doing something I've done countless times before, when I'm overtaken by a sense of plummeting descent. It's as if, unnoticed, right beside me, an abyss has opened up. It feels like I've stepped into it, quite oblivious, thinking it was just a continuation of the commonplace. When what I thought was solid ground opened without warning into unexpected space, I felt the shock of ambush. Despite the acceleration of falling, it's an abyss so deep that I have time to look around and get my bearings, examine what's rushing towards me from the depths.

Although such a sudden, vertiginous drop sounds perilous, in fact I'm safe enough. I'm being held, cradled by a rope that's wound around me and being paid out smoothly, length by length, with no indication it will ever be exhausted; it's threaded to a spool that's always replenished, that never seems to end. My sense of uncontrolled falling is only an illusion created by the sheer distance that I've covered in so short a time, the incredible depth I've got to when, only moments ago, I was standing on the surface of the everyday, enmeshed in time's usual minute-by-minute unfolding. Far from being in a doomed freefall towards death, I'm being lowered carefully. And I'm a willing partner in this jaw-dropping descent. I gladly let the rope be wound around me. There was no capture, no coercion, no push over the edge. This was a venture I embarked on of my own volition. However unnerving its destinations, this was a journey I was eager to make. In any case, I know I can return from it in an instant if I cast off the rope or exchange it for one of many others that lie coiled within easy reach.

I'm searching for a way to picture and explore something I'm so used to doing it's acquired an aura of invisibility. It's one of those ordinary — but really far from ordinary — accustomed things that's hidden in plain sight. I want to find an image that will arrest the mind, stop it from slipping into the automatic pilot of routine naming, assumption, and dismissal. Things done on a daily basis can lose their luster, become tarnished by repeated use, so that however shimmering with wonder their nature is, it becomes dulled, letting us dismiss as unremarkable what's really quite the opposite. Imagining myself lowered into a seemingly bottomless abyss on a kind of magic rope provides a way of looking afresh at what's so familiar there's a risk of not seeing it properly, of not appreciating the amazing thing it is.

Is this the best way to begin? Perhaps it would be better to abandon confusing talk of abysses and ropes in favour of a literal description, something like, "This morning I've been shown the stomach of a termite."

But stop there for a moment. We should not let past our guard "a literal description" without a body search of what it carries. Such locutions are expert at smuggling contraband across the borders of our notice, in this case the unexamined assumption of authority. Like other masquerades of virtuous accuracy — *the facts of the matter, the plain truth* — I suspect a *literal description* is rarely what it claims to be. Far from telling it like it is, rather than cutting cleanly to the heart of the matter and presenting it unadorned and rawly beating, such things are loyal to the codes of convention and convenience, which are rarely attuned to truthful apprehension. Such codes are closer kin to a kind of blindfolding, a simplification verging on obfuscation, than to anything that offers insight into the real nature of the things around us. It was precisely to avoid the blinkering of a literal description that I started with my image of falling into an abyss. But lest this image paints too puzzling a picture, let me give some background, state plainly what occasioned it, and why the unlikely sounding circumstance of being shown a termite's innards was such an awakening experience.

I've been reading Richard Dawkins's *The Ancestor's Tale*. The subtitle he's chosen describes the book as "A Pilgrimage to the Dawn of Life." Even saying no more than this may create a strong current of distraction. To prevent it drawing attention away from the path I wish to follow, let me acknowledge that Dawkins's name is often associated with the dispute between theists and atheists but say at once that this is something that doesn't concern me here. Whether the dawn of life was sparked by a creator deity, or, as Dawkins holds, by biochemical processes, is irrelevant to my purposes. I'll adopt neither a theistic nor an atheistic position and offer no comment on either perspective.

Towards the end of his book, Dawkins focuses on Darwin's termite (*Mastotermes darwiniensis*) in order to illustrate "the borrowing by greater creatures of the biochemical talents of lesser ones inside them." These Australian termites rely on "a rich gut fauna of microbes" to produce the enzymes that enable them to digest the cellulose and lignin in the wood they eat—a task the termites cannot perform themselves. As Dawkins puts it, the microbes "have become tools" in the termites' "biochemical toolkit." Or, to put it another way, Darwin's termites "farm microorganisms in their gut" and depend on the harvests they create there as surely as we depend on the harvests of our agricultural systems. The microorganisms in their turn receive a safe environment and a regular supply of food.

Dawkins focuses on one microorganism in particular, *Mixotricha paradoxa,* "a large protozoan, half a millimetre long or more." The gut of Darwin's termite is the sole habitat this species of protozoan occupies; it is the only place on Earth they're found. Just as the termites carry the unexpected cargo of *Mixotricha paradoxa* as an integral working part of their digestive system, so *Mixotricha* carries its own load of tiny essential life-forms. If you examine one, you'll find it contains "hundreds of thousands of bacteria." It depends on them for its survival just as much as the termites depend on *Mixotricha*. Some of these bacteria aid in the digestion of cellulose and lignin; others form tiny hairs that move together in such a coordinated manner that they provide their host protozoan with a means of propulsion via their synchronized movement.

In each termite's stomach, therefore, there is what Dawkins calls "a triple-decker dependency." The termites rely on microbes like *Mixotricha* to produce the enzymes they need to turn wood into a rich food source, whilst the *Mixotricha* in turn rely on their bacterial travelling companions for digestion and propulsion. In such cases, unsurprisingly, "it becomes quite tricky to draw the line between 'own' body and 'alien' body."

The story of the "triple-decker dependency" in a termite's stomach is amazing enough in itself. But what it points to is more amazing still. Namely, the way in which, some two billion years ago, it's thought the first eukaryote cells were formed. These are cells with a distinct nucleus that are larger and more complex than the simple, more ancient prokaryote cells, which had been until then the only living things on this planet. The cellular revolution that birthed the eukaryotes happened when larger cells engulfed smaller ones and, in time, the smaller ones became organelles within the larger entity, in the manner of the termites and *Mixotricha*, and *Mixotricha* and its bacteria. Traces of this ancient symbiotic congress can be seen most clearly in chloroplasts and mitochondria, which contain small amounts of genetic material that is different from that of their hosts. Dawkins spells out the implications nicely: "All our cells are like individual *Mixotrichs*, stuffed with bacteria which have become so transformed by generations of cooperation with the host cell that their bacterial origins are almost lost to sight."

In other words, they have become part of us.

I find it astounding—a source of humbling wonderment—that the complex cellular life of which we are one expression began with this ancient process of engulfment and symbiosis, and that we still bear traces of it in the deep structure of our bodies. The mitochondria in our cells constitute a kind of evidential watermark. Written indelibly into every micro-page that's bound together to make us there are subtle semaphore signals pointing back through the eons to this fusing together: the revolutionary symbiosis that birthed us. Without it, life would not have unfolded in the manner that it has. "The sublime grandeur of the real world," as Dawkins terms it, is truly awe-inspiring.

Given its grandeur, it's understandable that delving into life's ancient roots and contemporary manifestations can feel like plummeting into a vast abyss. In fact, it would be odd not to feel the conceptual ground of the ordinary giving way beneath our feet when faced with a saga unfolding over billions of years and still echoing loudly in the cellular building blocks that make protozoans, termites, and humans. There are incredible storylines written in detailed, beautiful profusion on the walls of the abyss—that is, on the fabric of time and space that's been colonized by life over such a stupendous period of years.

The Ancestor's Tale ranges over a plethora of creatures in its exploration of how species come and go, continue and perish, as life flourishes on Earth. Fascinating though his subject is, what I want to focus on is not life's origin and development but the means by which Dawkins documents it, the same means that anyone uses when they want to tell a story: language. It is language that constitutes the rope on which I've been lowered through the eons into an insect's innards. Without language I couldn't have journeyed to the lives of all the other creatures that *The Ancestor's Tale* examines.

The rope/language analogy first came to mind when I found myself taken into the gut of a Darwin's termite and shown what was there. It was as if, through his expert diction, Dawkins had woven together a cord of words on which readers could be lowered into the depths he was exploring. Knotting sentences together, braiding them into paragraphs, pages, chapters, I came to picture *The Ancestor's Tale* not as a thick book of 685 pages but as a strong rope of prose, down which I could slide into areas that would have been totally inaccessible to me without it.

Thinking of language as a rope provides a useful model by which to consider some of its functions. Like any model, it doesn't fit what it models exactly — it would be useless if it did. Instead, the creative mismatch that it offers suggests various metaphorical lenses through which what language does comes into clearer focus.

We use language so regularly, it is so much a part of us, that it's easy to forget how utterly remarkable it is. With very little effort, the sounds and shapes of words can be harnessed and made to carry incredible cargoes. Using only the twenty-six letters of the alphabet we can lasso any aspect of our experience and pull it towards the light of understanding. We can tie together disparate ideas to make new ones, rope together connections so that we've soon woven bridges across chasms of ignorance and incomprehension. We crack the whip of language and the world trots at its pace. Without the warp and weft of words I could not have led you here, nor could Dawkins have led me to the dawn of life. He in turn relied on the specialist discourse of scores of scientists talking to each other and recording their results. Language was the enabling factor for the portrait painted and shared in *The Ancestor's Tale.* Thought's propulsion relies on the cilia of ideas generated by scores of individuals, each rowing their coracle of understanding forward using the oars of words, each advance contributing to our progress.

Think of where language lets us go. Looking along the books on my shelves I could travel at a blink, just by turning a few pages, from the stomach of a termite to nineteenth-century Japan and the world as pictured by artists like Hokusai and Hiroshige; from there I might go to a study of the elements in the periodic table, or a life of Leonardo da Vinci; from there I might choose a history of Ireland or an examination of Buddhist theories of causation; there are books on birds' eggs, cave paintings, the secret life of trees, evolution, astronomy, geology, not to mention many works of poetry and fiction.

Sometimes now I think of every book as a coil of rope offering access to whatever subject it's concerned with. Language provides us with a means of extending the topography of our experience beyond its immediate, individual environs; it takes us to summits and crevasses, lets us cross oceans and deserts that are not part of the territory we occupy. By its means we can travel enormous distances both in time and space. The rope it spools out is more umbilical cord than inert cable. Through it come the nutrients of information, insight, interest, and amusement that we need. It allows us to share our lives with others as it allows them to put before us their perspectives and concerns. It helps us mesh together as a social species. It allows us to enter deep time, before any of us existed; it takes us to places we could never visit in the flesh, the stomach of a termite being just one example; it lets us see aspects of the world we would be blind to without it.

Looking along my bookshelves, I imagine the covers between the separate volumes dissolving and the ropes that each contains being spliced together until there's just a single massive line of corded words representing my whole reading life. It runs through the years, part nerve, part vein, part umbilical. The contours of sensibility it has created have done much to shape the landscape of the self. Without reading threaded through me, my life would have been significantly impoverished. And moving beyond the individual scale, where would we be as a species if all the words we've minted and exchanged were to be deleted from our cultural chromosomes and we fell silent again?

Do words provide the templates around which we weave our thoughts? Or do thoughts create the blueprints for the words we craft, so that we make them according to the invisibilities of intellection, thus giving public form to what is private, formless? Do thoughts crystallize around words, or words around thoughts? I suspect the two modalities are so intimately interlinked that to try to pull them apart would be to disfigure both and distort the way in which mind and language meld. The close connection between them is reminiscent of the symbiosis found within *Mixotricha paradoxa*, where it becomes hard to identify what is "own" and what is "alien" body. Given our reliance on it, language seems less a separate external presence than something that's become part of us. The verbal and the cognitive seem intimately interdependent. As linguistic beings we are surely the outcome of as epochal a revolution, as much of a turning point, as when eukaryotic cells emerged. Language seems like an integral part of us, something we've engulfed along the way and made our own. What we've learned to do with words is astonishing. We can talk about the constituents of atoms, catch in our marks upon a page the intricacies of photosynthesis, write about the age and likely origin of our planet, store in our paragraphs the history, psychology, and physiology of our species. Listen to us and you can hear a closeness of association, the symbolic become symbiotic, an intimate conjoining of life and language. Our course through history, indeed our very nature, is moulded by the sounds and shapes we daily forge in speech and writing.

Words allow us to navigate our way through life, but map is not territory. The ground we walk on is very different from our verbal accounts of it. It would be foolish to imagine there's a one-to-one correspondence between language and landscape, word and world. Our diction simplifies, omits, distorts, and highlights. We talk and write in patterns that mirror the isobars dictated by the weather of our needs. Language is obedient to the imperatives of desire and hunger, greed and curiosity, love and hatred, rather than to any objective lexicon that offers a verbatim tracing of what's there. But for all their limitations and distortions, words extend and enhance our cognitive reach, provide us with enzymes for understanding what, without them, we couldn't digest. Language is a kind of micro-fauna of the mind, the essential tool in our cognitive toolkit. We farm it in our diction and rely on the harvests that it offers. For all its familiarity, it is as incredible as anything that happens in the stomach of a termite.

Still Life with Witch-hazel

On the desk beside me, only six inches from the hand that's writing this sentence, there's a small glass vase. It's three-quarters full of water and holds two sprigs of witch-hazel. I cut them half an hour ago from the shrub in my garden. Each sprig is thickly prickled with ribbons of bright yellow blossom. Their spiky filaments cascade untidily. They look as if they're made from exploded daffodils whose flowers have been ripped into narrow shreds by the force of the blast. These remnant tatters erupt from multiple little fissures, miniature volcanoes, the craters nubbed like warts on the smooth wood of the stems.

It's a breezy January morning and I'm working in the attic, well wrapped up against the cold. There's frost on the ground outside and ice patterns spangle the skylight glass with a tracery of ghostly ferns. Every time a draft blows under the eaves it catches the witch-hazel's scent. Holding this cargo of fragrance, the wintry air bunches into an invisible fist that punches me repeatedly. This gentle assault by scent adds a potent olfactory dimension to the sprigs' insistent pulse of visible presence. Their color, perfume, and strange spiky shape combine to create an irresistible magnetism. It keeps tugging at my attention, pulling me back from daydreams to focus on the matter in hand.

Today I've turned word-artist and have set

myself a simple-sounding task: describe these sprigs of witch-hazel. What I want to do — experiment with doing — is a kind of alchemy in reverse. I want to transmute the gold of the witch-hazel's blossom into the black of print. The exercise raises, and stems from, a question that has long intrigued me. To what extent can words be cast in a manner so faithful to what they're describing that they allow readers to conjure in their minds the gold of actuality? Is it possible to rebuild from the marks I leave on page and screen the reality of what's here before me now: this vase of witch-hazel sitting on my desk?

In the way that visual artists doing still-life work become lightning conductors, earthing the electricity of what they see upon the paper's surface, so I want to be a conduit that allows the witch-hazel to flow from its actual presence in the vase into as perfect a verbal reflection of it as I can summon. My goal is to catch precisely the way in which these yellow-laden sprigs strike me. Pooled behind the dam wall of my sentences, can the reservoir of words I use to describe them slake the ancient thirst that communication addresses? I mean our desire to express experience, to chronicle what the world lays down upon us, to cross the precarious bridge between self and other so as to lay bare what touches us in our individual cells of consciousness, to share the secret interiority of sentience.

But a perfect verbal reflection is a hard — impossible? — thing to craft. Even just to talk about witch-hazel flowers already sounds like a wrong note. *Flower* leads the mind to the neat compactness of, say, a bluebell, foxglove, daisy, or rose, with petals forming well-defined orbs or cups or trumpets. The witch-hazel's ragged flowering is more like a random scattering of yellow threads, unwoven into any structure. When witch-hazel is in bloom, the leafless branches of the shrub are frosted all over with untidy straggles of yellow streamers. A first glance suggests chaotic profusion, hoards of shaggy golden ribbons cluttering the twigs. It looks as if the underlying wood has been slashed open, unzipped, letting these spidery innards spill out in all their gaudy disarray.

Like many first impressions, this one is mistaken. Closer examination reveals organization, a uniform pattern unsuspected by the eye's first scan, which is dazzled by the crazy ribboning of yellow. Look carefully and you'll see the separate flowers. Each one consists at root of a tiny quartet of reddish petals that encircle four anthers of the same hue, daintily tipped in yellow. The anthers stand guard around the almost invisible stigma, safely enclosed in their midst. Despite their color—which on the inside surface has an almost metallic sheen—these little rosy petals, in which the plant's sexual organs are so discreetly nestled, aren't seen at first. In part this is simply because they're so small, in part because they're sheathed in dusty-dull sepals holding them close to the twigs' camouflaging wood. But the main reason they're overlooked is because of what fountains from them.

In between each petal, rooted to the base flower, an integral part of it however separate they might seem, are long narrow filaments of yellow. Each flower sprouts four such filaments. They're about 1.5 cm long, 1 mm or so wide. The flowers grow in tight clusters of three, or more usually four, so each cluster sports twelve or sixteen filaments. They shower out in bright cascades and tangle with each other, fracturing any sense of singularity and hiding the demure fountains out of which they spring. It's hard to see the apparent chaos of these massed yellow filaments as parts of separate flowers. En masse their seeming frizz of disorder distracts from what makes it: the repeated pattern of the constituent individual blooms. The underlying blueprint, the way in which the design of every flower is replicated repeatedly, predictably, according to a standard format, is masked by the distracting exuberance of these multiple yellow outgrowths.

Edmund Husserl (1859–1938), the founding father of phenomenology, insisted that we should strive to reach "the things themselves," to see the world as it is, not through the distorting lenses of ideology or assumption. In a phenomenological perspective we would let what's there wash over our perception in all its original unfettered authenticity, the raw reality of its presence laid upon us in pristine condition, unencumbered by any crusting of presupposition, judgment, or evaluation. The voltage of existence would be allowed to touch us directly.

I was surprised when I found the ghost of Husserl playing around the witch-hazel blossoms. Like a pale, persistent moth around a flame, he kept catching my eye as I tried to formulate this word-picture. I read him years ago, but the fine detail of his ideas is long forgotten. Yet as soon as

I began to think about how to describe the witch-hazel, this phantom vestige of a dead philosopher came back to haunt me, urging me to adopt the radical purity of vision that was his Grail. Like the distracting rustle of moth wings caught in cobwebs, a trapped insect fluttering against some dusty window of the mind, *Zu den sachen selbst* (To the things themselves) kept muttering its whispered mantra.

In an effort to exorcise this Husserlian specter, or to obey its urging, my descriptions of the witch-hazel sprigs so far have not strayed beyond their fragrance and how they appear to the eye. But it would be dishonest to present this kind of pared-down perspective as more than the most fractional account. It omits mention of so much of what is there that, left to stand unqualified by this admission, it would be like a life-drawing where the artist has omitted several limbs.

Husserl's battle cry *Zu den sachen selbst* has a definite appeal, I don't deny it. It promises a kind of clarity, a sharpness of apprehension that flenses away inessentials, that cleaves simply to the clean lines of phenomena qua phenomena, sticking closely to the contours of things existing as they are, rather than getting drawn into the obscuring overlays of interpretation, theory, habit, and assumption. "To the things themselves" sounds like the determined wielding of a cognitive scalpel, something that can cut through the miasma of the secondary, get us to the heart of the matter. I'm drawn to the austere accuracy its incisions seem to offer.

But what *are* "the things themselves"? They're by no means as self-evident as a straightforward reading of phenomenology's motto makes it sound (nor was Husserl naïve enough to imagine that they were). What's given in experience is a complex, diverse, shifting cargo. It's not some single set of monotype perceptions that have somehow been besmirched by our illicit additions, so that all we have to do to restore their pure singularities is bracket out whatever we impose on them, thus allowing the revelation of their immediate touch upon our consciousness. Such perceptual simplicity, a dream of unsullied, virgin sensation, is very far from how things touch us with their presence.

When I look at the sprigs of witch-hazel in the vase on my desk, it's tempting to suppose that if I could provide a verbal transcription of what I see I'd be describing just what's there, obedient to the call to go "to the things themselves." But even supposing I could find words to fit exactly the "sensual astonishments" that have been thrown "upside down on the bloody membranes behind my eyeballs" (to borrow some lines from William Meredith's poem "Accidents of Birth"), it would be foolish, surely, to suppose that the visually literal (or its olfactory, tactile, or other sense parallels) represents more than a fraction of what's there. "The things themselves" contain far more than simple seeing can decipher.

If all I wanted to convey was the visual presence of the vase of witch-hazel on my desk—what meets the naked eye—I'd simply use a photograph. The old saying that "a picture is worth a thousand words" rings often in my mind, as it surely must in the minds of many writers, tolling like a funeral bell over the effectiveness of even the most precise verbal description. But what I want to catch is more than mere appearance, more than the manner in which things leave their mark upon the charts of shape and size and color by which our ocular cartography plots the data of visual input. Nor am I primarily concerned about what's laid down on the registers of the other senses: how the witch-hazel communicates its nature in terms of our perception of its textures, scents, whatever flavors it might possess, the noises the wind makes breezing through its leaves in autumn, or the slow, hypnotic sound of snow melting from its branches, sliding in slushy drips onto the still-unthawed ground beneath it. Such information is useful for initial orientation. It sets the scene, begins to triangulate the existence and nature of a thing; it fixes it in mind, pinpointing where it lies upon the modalities of our fivefold sensorium. But beyond these obvious, immediate characteristics of the thing itself, I'm interested in the way in which these yellow filaments of fragrant bloom have become part of the grammar of my life.

Like so many of the things around me witch-hazel has been absorbed into the vocabulary, the syntax of my identity; it's part of who I am. The things themselves are embedded in me and I in them. Accordingly, I can't describe them honestly by pretending the objectivity of supposed noninvolvement. Whenever I see these spiky yellow clusters now, they don't appear on some blank page where they're presented on their own, detached from everything that went before them, so that I only have to portray them thus, re-splendently simple in their isolation. Instead, they come already entwined with a cluster of memo-ries and associations. The DNA of their presence is formed by a double helix — strands of my story are braided together with the strands of what is there before me. I'm reminded of Paul Klee's observa-tion: "Art does not reproduce the visible, it *makes* things visible." Even supposing it was possible, I don't want to build some simulacrum of sight in words, a verbal mirror, reproducing on the page a one-to-one equivalence of what meets the eye in terms of light and shape and texture. Rather, I want to make visible what happens when I look at these sprigs of witch-hazel.

For me, their yellow tentacles reach out invis-ibly, instantaneously, and pull into mind a ritual I've often witnessed but haven't seen performed for years. I use *tentacles* deliberately. It's a stronger word than *filaments* for conveying a sense of some-thing that's alive. It's easy to lapse into the dull supposition that memory only holds what's dead and that there's an impassable barrier between the nows that face us and the thens we look back on but can no longer reach. This neat categorization of our experience draws an impermeable mem-brane between past and present. But the trans-action that's brokered every year whenever I see witch-hazel blossom doesn't fit this model with its strict territoriality, the watertight bulkheads that it closes in the mind. Witch-hazel floods me with something that's immediate, potent, vivid, pres-ent. There's no trace in it of two beats, of some-thing easily divided into separate moments, as if I could fold the map of my experience along some unerringly straight line, a temporal rift valley, that neatly quarantines today from yesterday. Instead, the blossom has a single pulse of impact. It acts like an instant catalyst, speeding a reaction that meets me, fait accompli, every winter when the shrubs come into bloom.

The tentacles of these flowers on my desk, fragrant beside me as I write, are already wrapped so closely around the blooms my mother cut in Ireland years ago that to pull the two apart would be to rupture a cognitive whole; it would fracture a singularity forged by the ancient alliance of perception-imagination-memory. To separate it into the kind of splinters favored by the imperative to neatly categorize and label would, to be sure, result in a simpler picture, and it would make the task of chronicling the things themselves appear more manageable. But any increase in easiness would be bought at the expense of shortchanging the impact witch-hazel actually has on me. To capture that requires the canvas of an essay; neither a photographer's camera nor an artist's brushwork could convey more than the most obvious contours of the landscape into which it takes me, lush with its foliage of feeling, memory, and connection, a terrain densely threaded with a network of paths that crisscross repeatedly between past and present.

An important feature of my childhood home in Lisburn, a northern Irish town not far from Belfast, was an elegant hall clock, the kind horologists refer to as a Vienna regulator. It was one of those things that made a deep-enough impression that it feels permanent, as if it had leaned its weight against me for so long it left an indentation on the psyche. The clock possessed what I can best describe as a kind of totemic aura; it was surrounded by its own atmosphere—an invisible penumbra of power emanated from it, creating a force field that affected us all. It was one of the centers of gravity in the house, exerting an influence on the daily orbits that we followed. Fixed to the wall to the left of the front door, the clock was an integral part of the signature of home. Winding it up was one of the ritual pleasures of childhood. I had to be lifted up to do so by my father until I'd grown tall enough—an epochal moment—to reach it myself.

Opening the wooden-framed glass door, fitting the key into the hole in the white-enameled clock face with its black Roman numerals, the ratchet noise as the key was being turned, and the way the single drop mechanism pulled up the cylindrical brass weight—these were important elements in the little domestic routines that ordered our lives back then. Imbued with the custom of repeated practice, these actions became part of our family's traditions so that they still mark my recollection of those days. The carved female head at the top of the clock case, set into the finial and made of the same dark wood as the clock's impressive chrysalis (mahogany? ebonized walnut? rosewood?), was like some tutelary spirit, a personification of time and place. She looked down on us benignly as the minutes ticked away.

The clock has become so close-shackled in my mind with witch-hazel blossom that whenever I see its yellow filaments, they seem to have invisibly inscribed on them the slow ticktock I know so well, together with the gentle rhythmic swing of the pendulum and the face of that familiar carved wooden head. This close connection means that whenever I encounter witch-hazel now a sense of being back there in the hall, presided over by the clock, is immediately kindled.

What led to this fusing of two such unrelated things, a clock made in Austria or Germany sometime in the nineteenth century and a winter-flowering plant whose cut twigs made a splash of scent and color in a house in County Antrim every year of my childhood? The clock took up much of the space on a narrow column of wall between two rooms. Below it was a small wooden table, its top little more than a foot square. Scarves were kept in its single shallow drawer, but the table's main function was to provide a platform on which to display a cluster of my mother's cloisonné ornaments, together with a small vase of flowers. What the vase held varied according to the season, but in January it was invariably the yellow of witch-hazel. This gave way to snowdrops, dwarf narcissi, primroses, fritillaries, grape hyacinths, roses — whatever blooms the garden offered as the year progressed. The vase on the table acted as a kind of natural timepiece, marking the seasons' turning. Its semaphore of blooms sounded a less regular beat than the clock's steady metronome, but its different key and variable tempo signaled time's passing just as surely as the rhythm ticking out with mechanical exactitude above it.

Because it marked the close of one year and the start of another, because of its scent, because of the strikingly unusual shape of the flowers, the witch-hazel always made a particular impression.

It was as if it and the clock conspired together to strike a special annual chime: the first flowers after Christmas. Also significant, I think, was the fact that the sprigs cut for the vase were tall enough for the yellow filaments to brush the bottom of the clock case, making a physical connection between them, a vein or an umbilical cord through which each bled something of itself into the other. These factors, and no doubt others I'm unaware of, meant that a close coupling was forged so that clock and witch-hazel became inseparably conjoined.

It's easy for familiarity to skew a sense of time. Because she did it every year for as far back as I can remember, my mother's annual ritual of cutting the fragrant yellow-spiked twigs has imbued witch-hazel with a sense of long-established presence that its history doesn't warrant. No doubt the clock helped to foster this false chronology, given the extent to which it was spliced to the plant by close association. The hall clock was such a landmark in my childhood that it seemed always to have been there. Witch-hazel has come to share that same air of permanence, something whose roots stretch back far enough they make it seem an unquestioned given. In a way, both seemed as old as time itself, because I'd never experienced life without them.

As a species witch-hazel is ancient, true enough. Push back through the centuries in which it's grown and you enter a timeline that can be calibrated in millions of years. In the same way that a maze of microscopic detail underlies the lulling integument of simple shapes that meet the eye —

the intricate arrangements of the cells and molecules and atoms that constitute the deep structure of each twig, of every flower—so beneath the shallow waters of duration that we measure with the manageable metrics of clock time lie eons that dwarf our usual scales. But in an Irish context, as short a time ago as my mother's childhood, witch-hazel would have been a novel rarity only just becoming known. The variety she favored and planted in our garden wasn't available for sale in British nurseries until as recently as 1902.

Witch-hazel belongs to the family *Hamamelidaceae.* There are four species in America and two in Southeast Asia, one Chinese, one Japanese. It was an American species, *H. virginiana,* that was first introduced to Britain. It's uncertain who was responsible for bringing the plant across the Atlantic. Peter Collinson (1694–1768), a London-based Quaker who had connections with his co-religionists in Pennsylvania, is often credited as the key figure here. An acquaintance of Collinson's, fellow Quaker and plant enthusiast John Fothergill (1712–80), is also sometimes mentioned as being instrumental in establishing the plant in English gardens. Its medicinal use by Native American tribes soon spread to the settlers and then to Europe. It became so common as a mild antiseptic, lineament, and balm, and as an ingredient in cosmetics, that it's in that form—rather than as a flowering plant—that most people encounter witch-hazel today. I'm not sure when the first specimens of *H. virginiana* started to appear in Irish gardens. Even assuming it was not long after the plant's appearance in England, that means witch-hazel can only claim a presence in Ireland of less than three centuries.

But the plant my mother grew, whose flower-laden twigs appeared each year on the table below the clock, wasn't *H. virginiana*. The modest pale-yellow blooms of this species are small enough to miss, particularly as it flowers as early as September, before all the leaves have fallen. The perfume of *H. virginiana* is modest too; it doesn't pack the strident punches of fragrance that hit me from the sprigs in the attic. My mother favored the Chinese variety of witch-hazel, *Hamamelis mollis,* whose introduction to Britain dates only from the late nineteenth century. It's one of around five hundred varieties of plants brought to the country by Charles Maries (1851–1902), a plant collector employed by what was then one of Britain's best-known nurseries, James Veitch and Son of Chelsea, London. Maries made several expeditions to Southeast Asia. He found the witch-hazel in the Chinese province of Jiujiang, in the vicinity of Mount Lushan, in 1878.

When Charles Maries stumbled on witch-hazel growing in China, the hall clock that I know so well would have been ticking away in another house in Ireland. I don't know its history in detail, but I do know that it was as potent a presence in my father's childhood as it was in mine. He remembered it as a key feature of his family home in Londonderry. In the same way that winding it was an important ritual in my growing up, being lifted to do so until tall enough to reach the clock

face myself, so my father recalled doing likewise
with his father. He was continuing a tradition
that had left its imprint on him (as it had likewise
done with his father before him). As the pendulum weight dropped slowly down until elevated
again by winding, as the hands crept round the
clock face, lives edged forward year by year—
Charles Maries's, my father's, my grandfather's,
my great-grandfather's, countless unmet others
in China, Ireland, and all the area between. When
his parents died and their Londonderry home was
sold, my father inherited the clock and brought
it to the house in Lisburn. The steady ticktock of
the clock sounded throughout his life. He and my
mother have been dead for years now, the Lisburn
house not only sold but razed to the ground and
another house built in its place. The hall table and
the vase for flowers were given away or lost a
long time ago, but the clock still ticks its rhythm
through the days. Today it hangs on a wall in my
brother's house, the familiar carved wooden head
looking down on the lives of another family. Eventually, I suppose, one of his children will continue
the tradition.

In my childhood home in Lisburn the clock
was located just inside the front door. We passed
it and the table each time we came into the house,
each time we left. The clock's figurehead was there
above us as if on a ship's prow, watching with its
sightless eyes as our life-voyages unfolded in that
place. Pendulum swing, regular winding, hands
pointing to the Roman numerals, the beat of our
chronology's familiar systole-diastole placed a human overlay, a palimpsest of simple numbers we
could work with, upon the incalculable measures

that constitute time's amplitude.

I wonder what flowers were the first ones my mother cut to display here when, newlywed, she and my father moved into the house. On cold nights when temperatures plummet, witch-hazel's yellow streamers curl inwards to protect the plant's generative organs. As she and my father pulled the bedding closely around them against the winter chill, was their snuggling down silently echoed in the garden as the witch-hazel's filaments curled in? What sprays of bloom stood on the hall table as the intimate pollination of their lovemaking took place? When my newborn form was carried into the house for the first time, did the vase on the table—since it was early February—hold witch-hazel, did the fragrance touch me, or would it have been snowdrops by then? Some thirty years later, when my father's coffin was taken out, an awkward maneuver in the hall's tight space, I remember yellow roses, some petals fallen on the polished wood. What were the last flowers my mother ever arranged on the stage of that small table? At what point as she cut witch-hazel twigs did she ask the question I now ask myself? How many more times will I see witch-hazel blossom, smell its fragrance; how many seasons have I left? And paralleling these questions about individual finitude, how long since the very first witch-hazel flowered? Who first saw it? Who will be the last human ever to sense its scent? When will witch-hazel go extinct? And between the tick of its first occurrence, the tock of its final withering, what will happen in the world?

The seeds Charles Maries collected in 1878 almost didn't take. Only one grew to maturity, and staff at Veitch's Coombe Wood Nursery mislabeled it as *H. japonica,* or Japanese witch-hazel. By good fortune the curator of the Royal Botanic Gardens at Kew, George Nicholson, corrected the mistake when he visited the nursery in 1898. He saw the plant for what it was and recognized its qualities. Chinese witch-hazel is notable for its large, bright yellow blooms and the strength of their perfume. The flowers appear only after all the leaves have fallen. This, coupled with their size and hue, makes *H. mollis* far more striking than the demure-by-comparison *H. virginiana* (which today is often used as rootstock onto which *H. mollis* is grafted). Charles Maries's wanderings for Veitch and Son affected numerous gardens, including three of mine: my childhood one in Ireland; the garden I planted out in Wales, where my own children first saw witch-hazel; and the garden in Scotland where I'm living now, from where I cut the sprigs for the vase that's sitting on my desk. Each garden not only had a witch-hazel but, in each case, growing just a stone's throw from it, another of Maries's discoveries, *Magnolia stellata,* whose white starburst blossoms start to come out just as the witch-hazel's are fading.

In a verbal sketch of witch-hazel, some information is already imparted automatically even before going any further than bestowing names. *Hamamelis* means "together with fruit," pointing to the way the flowers appear on the branches at the same time as they bear maturing fruit from the previous year. *Mollis* simply means "soft" and refers to the texture of the leaves, which have an almost suede-like quality. But names also carry the potential to mislead, to nudge the mind along pathways that are at odds with the true north of what's there. *Witch* inevitably activates the word's primary referent: "someone, especially a woman, supposed to have magical powers, usually, but not always, malevolent in nature." But this meaning has nothing to do with the *witch* in witch-hazel. It derives from Old and Middle English terms that refer to a quality of the wood — *wiche* or *wice* — meaning bendable or pliant (terms that also supply the root for *wicker*).

Two misnamings cloud the picture. *Hazel* came about when the first American settlers, being reminded of the hazels they knew from home, gave this name to a newly encountered plant on the other side of the Atlantic. It looked to them the same. Whether real similarity or the nostalgic prompts of homesickness caused them to name witch-hazels thus, in fact the plants are not close relatives of the *Corylus avellana* hazel that's indigenous to England, with which they would have been so familiar. Of course, the name *hazel* also carries a cargo of its own. The word is of Anglo-Saxon origin and comes from *haesel* or *haesl,* denoting what Edward L. Step (in *Wayside and Woodland Trees*) calls "a baton of authority, from the use of its rods in driving cattle and slaves."

The second misnaming comes in the way in which a completely different tree, wych-elm (*Ulmus glabra*) is sometimes referred to as witch-hazel. But the *wych* in this case has a different derivation. It's thought to stem from the fact that this tree's wood was once used to make the chests called in ancient England *wyches, hucches,* or *whycches.* Alternatively, the use of elm to make troughs and pipes for holding and conveying brine from salt springs (*wyches*) may account for the *wych* in wych-elm.

When we go to the things themselves with language, we take with us what words already carry in their sounds and shapes. Our utterance is always haunted by the voices of those who have spoken before us. Language is pooled with the hidden sinkholes of history; it ripples with the currents of half-remembered associations and secret connections. Its verbal genealogies and bloodlines bestow a dowry that's not always wanted on all the marriages of sense we try to make.

Words, unlike drawn lines, come prepackaged with a load of meaning. Scratch their surface and connections proliferate as the warp and weft of language starts to knit together, word to word to word, enveloping in their web whatever we wish to talk about. When we pull in our spoken/written nets we land some shoal of understanding on our deck. But whether we have caught the things we sought or something else isn't always easy to determine. Words possess an inbuilt angle of refraction. Spearing with them is an art that always issues in some degree of miss.

The question is, how wide of the target are we shooting?

I'm reminded of the great haiku master Basho's advice: "Let not a hair's breadth separate your mind from what you write." Like Husserl, he gives primacy to the things themselves. A well-cast hai-ku lets them speak to us directly, almost without intermediaries. Stripped down to the bare bones of concision, the breath of a moment is allowed to brush our skin with its unworded presence. As the main authority on haiku in English, R. H. Blyth, once said, "Haiku take away as many words as possible between the thing and the reader." Does this mean I should score out all I've written here, dismiss it as a sketch that hasn't worked, an ab-errant haiku whose monstrous proportions need to be pruned back hard, reduced to just seventeen syllables? Instead of an essay, should I make my words into a streamlined three-line trident, throw it into the waters of experience, attempt to spear the salmon of witch-hazel that's swimming so en-ticingly, so elusively, in the moments of my seeing it?

Perhaps.

But since the task I set myself was to describe the witch-hazel in the glass vase on my desk, it's worth remembering what description is beyond its bland definition: "an account of anything in words." Mark Doty has some helpful comments to make here. In *The Art of Description* he says:

> What descriptions — or good ones, any-way — actually describe is conscious-ness, the mind playing over the world of matter, finding there a glass various and lustrous enough to reflect back the complexities of the self that's doing the looking.

I agree with Doty that "to the degree it gives us not just the world but the inner life of the witness," description is an art rather than some slavish reflection obedient point-by-point to what is there. And the best description "makes meaning in itself, building an argument about the nature of the real." Moreover, in the same way that the nature of description may not be what we commonly assume, so with still life. In her history of the genre Sybille Ebert-Schifferer describes it as "uniquely poised between reality and illusion."

It's not as if the thing itself is one single graspable entity, some great white whale of obvious dimensions that could be pinned down with a decisive thrust of the phenomenologist's harpoon. It's more that the sprigs of witch-hazel in the vase on my desk create a kind of reef that provides a habitat for a whole array of perceptions, memories, ideas, and associations. There are wrecks in the waters around it, rusty anchors, brightly colored fish, a Vienna wall clock floating past ruddered with its familiar tick. Remembered voices, faces, hints, suggestions, fears, and dreams can be glimpsed among the tangles of seaweed. The rich ore of microscopic structure, and the biochemical subtleties they contain, hints at their presence as the water's currents swirl and change, sluicing their way across the shallows of the present, corkscrewing out of the abysses of deep-time, trenched and unfathomable, with which the seabed of each moment is underlain. Simply to focus on the sprigs themselves as isolated phenomena would leave upon the page no accurate word-sketch from which experience could be rebuilt, no glimpse of the wealth of things that surface in my mind along with the yellow filaments. It would only offer an empty shell, something gutted, hollowed out, no more than a skeletal remnant, the residue of what's there. To conduct such a violent reduction might be a kind of phenomenology, but it would also be to purge the intricate ecosystems that interlace between us and the world, creating in their delicate whorls of interconnection the miracle of consciousness.

Just as no drawing can ever catch completely the richness of its subject, so the sprigs of witch-hazel likewise elude more than a fractional word-portrait, a provisional pinning-down, one possible perspective among many that could be drawn. Apart from everything else, each of our encounters with the world, however commonplace they seem, contains an element of what Zen Buddhists call *ichi-go ichi-e* (one time, one meeting), the fact that every moment is a once-in-a-lifetime thing; it will never be repeated, never come again in just that manner, in the exact same form. So even though witch-hazel carries the kind of cargo I've outlined, who knows how it may strike me on some other breezy January day? Such uniqueness alone would render suspect any claim to have fashioned a facsimile, whether in words or images. Even supposing such a thing could somehow convey the weight of the cargo bound to the yellow filaments, show the way in which the blossom is a portal opening into intricacies of structure and duration that dwarf all our calibrations, the uniqueness of "one time, one meeting" would demand that we throw away our sketch and start again.

To imagine that a writer or an artist could become a conduit that simply channels the things themselves, exactly as they are, into marks upon a page would be to fail to grasp the nature of the media they use and the relationship in which those media stand to whatever they're applied to. It would also be to fundamentally misunderstand the nature of the real, to imagine that somehow it's "out there" and we're "in here," and that keeping to the fastness of ourselves we can be apart from the world and render its likeness with clinical detachment. But the sprigs of witch-hazel six inches from the hand that's writing this essay are in fact at no such safe remove. They thread through me, become entangled with my nerves and veins, so that when I write them into being on the page the spoor of my own blood tints whatever marks I leave. What's written can only convey a very little of what's there; catching "the things themselves" is no more than a dead philosopher's dream. In formulating our repeated flawed descriptions of being, the best we can do is keep in mind what's needed to improve them, to make less inadequate their inevitable imperfections. Mark Doty puts the matter well: "To be better at description, we have to work at attentiveness." Or as another poet, Mary Oliver, said in an apothegm with which Basho would agree: "To pay attention, this is our endless and proper work."

Fitting In

Essay writing is reflective; it doesn't just want to recount things that happened, but contemplate what they mean, and often what they mean is really about how they fit into the pattern, which is how the particular connects to the general.

—REBECCA SOLNIT

Most weeks I walk here, often several times; it's become a favorite haunt—so much so that the pattern of the place has left an imprint on my memory, a kind of film of familiarity. This film is thickened, reinforced, each time I revisit and see these surroundings through it one more time. I've come to recognize the lie of the land here with the minuteness of detail afforded by repetition. The little lineaments of path and grass and trees and flowers have become like the handwriting of a friend, instantly identified as theirs for all the day-to-day variation brought about by changes of weather and season. This means that anything that's new stands out, rupturing the gauze of what's known with the novelty of its intrusion. Whatever breaks the pattern I've come to associate with here draws the eye with the magnetism of unexpectedness.

To begin with, what I saw simply registered as something that did not fit in, a deviation from these norms of familiarity I'd grown used to. This initial impression of it as something alien, something that did not belong, was of course mistaken—in fact a bizarre misapprehension. But my error in seeing thus what's actually an integral and indelible part of the pattern only dawned on me later. At the moment of first encounter it just seemed out of place, a rip in the radar of what I was anticipating. It immediately drew my notice.

Clearly there was something on the path ahead, a shape I'd not seen on any of my many walks. In the middle of the gravelled surface, just a stone's throw from me, I saw something solid and dark colored. Every now and then it moved, with an odd jerky motion. No doubt because this favorite walk is in a botanical garden, rich with all sorts of exotic plants, I toyed with the idea of the flat surface of the path having ruptured, splitting open to reveal a strange, emergent bloom that was now swaying unsteadily in the breeze. But as I got closer, the shape became more animal- than plant-like. So despite the horticultural setting, I looked for a different image to lasso and label it, to draw it into the realm of what I recognized. Still at some distance from it, I decided the most likely hypothesis was that it was a rabbit, and—since this would account for its sporadic lurches—probably one infected with myxomatosis, or in some other way afflicted. But soon I saw that my initial attempt to parse this unexpected presence into the grammar of the known was some way off the mark. It was in fact two creatures locked together in what was for one a lethal and the other a life-sustaining embrace.

I'd happened on a sparrowhawk kill. It must have been only seconds before I appeared on the scene that the hawk had brought down the wood-pigeon it was standing on in the middle of the path. Pigeons are about the largest prey sparrowhawks will attempt. Usually, as in this case, such attacks are made by female hawks, which are significantly bigger than the males. Sparrowhawks mostly take their prey on the wing, typically by ambush or after a short pursuit. Sometimes the first strike of the talons or the impact of hitting the ground will kill the prey outright. But not in this case; the pigeon was still obviously alive.

I left the path and approached on the grass, slowly and quietly, using the cover provided by some fuchsia bushes. The hawk must have seen me — their eyesight is acute — but it didn't want to leave its prize. I was no doubt dismissed as a lumbering irrelevance, of little more concern to it than a plant. Masterful aeronauts, if the hawk needed to escape it could have done so with a couple of easy wingbeats. Eventually I stopped only a few feet away, stood quite still, and watched it feed, plucking at the pigeon's breast with its hooked beak. Downy feathers flew around the hawk's head like the seeds from a violently shaken dandelion. As they increased in number they revealed shocking glimpses of red flesh beneath their cushioning. Talons sunk in its quarry, the hawk scythed and tugged with its beak. It was soon tearing out little gobbets of bloody meat.

How long did the pigeon survive this treatment? It's hard to know for sure when it crossed the line from life to death, but from any empathetic view it was not nearly soon enough. Its wings beat uselessly on the ground, making it sound as if someone was sweeping the gravel with flurries of short, frantic strokes. I hoped rather than believed that some of the movements were just the reflex actions of a corpse, nerves and muscles triggered into automatic spasm that was unfeeling, merely mechanical, rather than being the desperation of a live thing trying to escape. But I know hawks well enough to know they are not merciful. As Ian Newton puts it in his careful study of this raptor, "To the sparrowhawk, it does not matter whether their victim is killed immediately, only that it stays reasonably still while being eaten."

The raw violence of the kill instilled the moment with a dramatic aura. As a spectator I was both enthralled and appalled by the performance I was witnessing. Utterly riveted, even if disgusted, my attention was held completely. Perhaps I'd soon have tired or grown sickened by it if, shortly after I stopped to watch, other players hadn't appeared on the scene to add the spice of uncertainty about the outcome. A magpie landed on the path and scolded loudly. It hopped closer and closer to the hawk and its quarry, warily but with determination. Then it darted in and pecked at the pigeon, which flapped in response to this new source of torment. The hawk tried to take off but couldn't get airborne with the weight and awkwardness of its weakly struggling victim. The magpie darted in again and pecked. No doubt alerted by its scolding cries, two more magpies appeared. Would this trio of scavengers rob the hawk of its kill? Finally, with immense effort, the hawk flew heavily away, the pigeon's now motionless weight grasped in its talons like some gigantic bomb that was almost as big as the aircraft it was slung under. Pulled down by its cargo, the hawk disappeared at low altitude into the trees and undergrowth bordering the path, pursued by the raucous magpies. I'm not sure how things ended.

Should I have intervened? Chased the hawk away as soon as I saw it, tried to save the pigeon? The thought crossed my mind but I didn't act on it, in part because this was a rare opportunity to watch a sparrowhawk at close quarters. They're not often seen in the open. J. A. Baker, author of *The Peregrine* (1967) — perhaps the most lyrical account ever written of a bird of prey — describes sparrowhawks as "hard to find and harder to see," while James Macdonald Lockhart, in *Raptor: A Journey through Birds* (2016), notes how they rely on concealment: "The sparrowhawk must always be just out of sight; and that is where you will find one." To find one in plain sight was too good an opportunity to miss by chasing it away. But I also realized that if I'd scared it off, I'd have been left with a fatally injured pigeon and the question of whether, and how, to dispatch it. I knew that as it stood on its prey the hawk's talons would not have been idle. Looking at how the killing happens, Ian Newton notes that as well as the lethal role of impact, prey is also squeezed in the hawk's feet and that the two largest claws "can each penetrate more than a centimetre." The pigeon could not have survived such multiple stabbings, pistoned deeply into it as the hawk stood hooked and anchored to its body.

The risk of starting as I have done with a description is that it focuses on the immediacies of vision. What met my eye in those few minutes was certainly arresting, but to concentrate solely on the scene-as-seen would be to miss its weightier dimensions. The problem with attempting a visual transcription—casting words to give details of the event I watched unfolding—is that it ignores the questions that clamor noisily behind the muting labels of our ordinary vocabulary. I'm not so much interested in what happened between sparrowhawk, pigeon, and magpies as in what that moment of their interaction says about the world I live in, what I can learn from it, what light it sheds on the nature of things.

Indeed, I'm curious about what *counts* as a moment in the first place. What criteria do we use to draw the boundaries around such a limited singularity, separating it from the flow of time that every moment is part of? When does one moment become another? When does one end, another one begin, and what constitutes the boundaries between them? The moment that, for convenience, I'll refer to as *the sparrowhawk kill I witnessed* maybe started when I first noticed the unexpected shape on the path ahead of me and ended when the hawk flew out of sight, closely pursued by the magpies. It lasted four or five minutes at most. But one of the things that intrigues me is the way those few minutes are part of something incomparably greater. They are bordered by — spliced to — eons of duration.

Out of time's torrent, the onward rush of centuries in which everything is borne along, we map the tiny areas that concern us: the minutes, hours, and days, the months and years that measure out our lifespans. And within these human-scale cartographies we pick out the fragments that catch our eye, like *the sparrowhawk kill I witnessed*. To pick something out suggests that we can get a grip on it, that it offers cognitive handholds, that there's something about it that allows us to lift it clear, consider it in isolation, and affix names, descriptions, labels. In this manner we moor such manageable fragments to the quayside of the known with the ropes of language. But such moorings are far less secure than I once believed them to be. However much I try to pin down what happened in a description, I feel *the sparrowhawk kill I witnessed* tugging at the ropes of words with a strength that mocks their breaking strength.

Meaning-making, that unnoticed industry we're perpetually engaged in, the process by which we make the world make sense to us, depends on cutting down the gargantuan scale of time and space that faces us into moments, objects, events, relationships, making stories that are sized to fit the constraints of consciousness and the limits of our language. But as I watched the sparrowhawk, thought about it, tried to write about it later, it felt as if the moorings that I'd used were coming loose. What I'd described pulled on the ropes of language, tugging against their restraint, drifting heavily away from the harbor of ordinary particularities. I was reminded of lines in Ted Hughes's poem "Hawk Roosting":

> It took the whole of Creation
>
> To produce my foot, my each feather

The moment that caught my eye may have lasted only a few minutes but it somehow reeked of ancientness. The players on the gravel path are creatures whose individual existences are brief enough, but they are also expressions of forms and processes that have taken millions of years to develop. I'm not sure why, but those four or five minutes of brutal, small-scale drama pointed insistently beyond themselves to a chasm of chronology that dwarfed them. Though in one sense I took it as one vivid moment with a beginning and an end that I could grasp, features I could catch in words, in another it felt as if it pulled me into time's flow where such ordinary calibrations are swept away by a current that none of our symbols can map. It took the whole of Creation, all of time up to that fleeting point, to generate *the sparrow-hawk kill I witnessed.*

The way the moment moved from one scale to another, taking me from watching birds encountered on a walk to thinking of the centuries that lay behind them, the astonishing backstory that roots them in the flow of time, reminded me of Montaigne's insistence that movement is built into the DNA of everything we experience. As he puts it, in his essay "On Repentance":

> The world is but a perennial movement.
>
> All things in it are in constant motion—

> the earth, the rocks of the Caucasus, the
> pyramids of Egypt — both with the com-
> mon motion and their own. Stability
> is nothing but more languid motion.

In other words, everything is in transition; movement is indelibly ingrained in the deep structure
of things. Time's passing leaves its watermark
everywhere, fusing then and now and next together in an unstoppable flow that undermines
all the apparent fixities of our halting vocabulary.
As a corollary to his recognition of this constant
motion, the fact that change is an integral and intimate part of the fabric of things, Montaigne notes
the key characteristic of his writing: "I do not portray being; I portray passing." And for Montaigne,
passing didn't just mean "passing from one age
to another," the kind of ordered steps that can be
imagined as we progress from year to year, following a sequence that's sufficiently gradual we
can foster the illusion of static points along the
way. Rather, he had in mind something more intense, more all-pervasive: namely, the passing that
occurs "from day to day, from minute to minute,"
the ceaseless flow that animates everything, the
bloodstream that feeds existence its vital oxygen of
time. *The sparrowhawk kill I witnessed* was indelibly
branded with the mark of movement; the currents
of passing were rippled through it, leaving their
wave marks on the sand of its substance, making
it at once seem transient and ancient, laden with
a temporal load as hard to lift as the pigeon was
for the hawk, yet light enough to vanish in a few
heartbeats.

Just as a theater stage is emptied of performance once the actors have left it, so despite the drama played out on the path, little trace of it remained once the birds had flown. Apart from a few white, downy remnants, the cloud of plucked feathers was soon dispersed by the wind. What little bloodstaining reddened the ground was washed away by rain and morning dew. Whatever remained of the corpse after the hawk and magpies had had their fill would, I knew, be rendered down by insects and bacteria. The bones and feet would last longest, but their mute testimony to the existence of the slain pigeon would quickly enough turn into anonymous detritus as they rotted back into the humus in whatever patch of undergrowth they were abandoned. Soon the lie of the land, the lineaments of path and trees and flowers, would return to normal, would again look just as my familiarity with them expected them to look, everything fitting neatly into its accustomed place.

What lasted for longer than I expected were the marks left on the gravel by the pigeon's frantic wingbeats. The scuff marks were still visible a week later, the stones swept by the wing strokes into a pattern of little ridges and gullies. Each time I saw that pattern, it seemed like a kind of hieroglyph, a fragment of writing incised upon the ground. Although I knew its provenance well enough, it struck me as a kind of rune or glyph — a symbol that held some meaning. Trying to decipher it I thought of monks sweeping a Zen gravel garden, brushing the stones into patterns in a rhythmic, meditative action that could still and focus the restless psyche, shut out distraction, allow insight to be nurtured. What state of mind, I

wondered, does the pigeon's gravel brushing foster, what insights are sparked by the whirlpool
of currents that created these particular patterns?
What can be read from this shard of ancient alphabet that contains such a desperate meditation on
mortality, written in a creature's very lifeblood
with the quills of its final movements?

It's easy to dismiss uncomfortable truths as
fanciful, or label my reaction to the pigeon's end
as mere anthropomorphism, to think I'm making
mountains out of the molehill of this little event,
or that I'm simply misreading what I encountered.
I don't much warm to the exegesis of experience
that took shape as I tried to read the pattern inked
into the canvas of the path by the pigeon's wingbeats—a pattern that carried something of the
same authority as a confession given in extremis.
But I'm wary of discounting an interpretation simply because I don't like it.

Every time I walked past the site of the killing in the days that followed, the marks on the
path brought back to mind the pigeon's horrible
demise—the hawk clamped to it like some mer-
ciless, mad-eyed surgeon conducting a brutal
transplant, feeding its own life with the pigeon's
vital substance. Each time the scene came back to
mind I knew it wasn't just a one-off happening, a
disruption to the familiar patterns I was used to
in this tranquil place. Far from being something
alien that did not fit in, it was, rather, an integral
and essential part of things. Whatever alphabet
the hawk is part of, whatever letter it stands for,
is written into me and into every other creature.

We speak the same syllables of existence, sign the same semaphore of blood and being, talk the same dialect of breath and butchery.

Whatever spells my end is unlikely to have the savage beauty of a hawk, and I hope will be gentler in its dispatch than talon-stab and hooked-beak slash and pull, but the result will be the same. The spirit of the raptor, whether it takes the form of accident, disease, attack, or old age, hovers above every creature, poised to descend in whatever moment holds its end. My body—all bodies—will be as completely dismantled as the pigeon's. I will leave no more trace than it did on the life paths that I've walked. The little drama of my passing will leave the scuff marks of my struggle for a fleeting moment before they vanish and time moves on, its flow containing every pigeon's hatching, every human's, every hawk's, together with the nullity of nonbeing as we all pass into nothingness.

According to Ortega y Gasset, metaphor "is probably the most fertile power" we possess. Along the same lines, Jonathan Miller suggests that "since finding out what something is is largely a matter of finding out what it is like," it follows that "the most impressive contribution to the growth of intelligibility has been made by the application of suggestive metaphors." What suggestive metaphors can help us establish what a sparrowhawk kill is like and so edge it into the territory of intelligibility? It's easy enough to compare it to other predatory occurrences: a pride of lions feeding on a wildebeest, a killer whale catching a seal, a wasp bringing down a butterfly in flight and eating it, a spider with a fly. But these have the flavour more of equivalents than elucidations; the likenesses they offer are too close to take us forward. What's needed is an image that stands at enough of a distance from *the sparrowhawk kill I witnessed* to lever it into a different focus.

But I'm at a loss to find one. Nothing seems to fit the niche that yearns and beckons for a meaning that might gentle things into something more palatable to our taste than the prospect of disintegration and dispersal.

The philosopher of language J. L. Austin once described *like* as a word that provides the linguistic equivalent of being able "to shoot round corners." I'd like to find a way of shooting round — seeing beyond — the corner of *the sparrowhawk kill I witnessed,* but no fitting likeness comes to mind. Metaphor may be the most fertile power we possess, as Ortega y Gassett says; it may play the crucial role in fostering intelligibility that Miller suggests. But it can gain no purchase here. This seems less like a corner we might learn to shoot round than a cul-de-sac we're trapped in. No comparison I can think of provides sufficient traction to gain purchase on the sheer walls of annihilation that surround us — the encirclement of every living thing by the precipice of finitude. Is there any way to shoot round with sense the message we find written on time's gravel? Lives brush patterns there that seem stark indeed in what they tell us: that eventually, inevitably, we're all subject to mortality's talons, that the moments we occupy will one day evict us, and that our absence from the world, not our presence in it, is overwhelmingly the larger reality.

Every moment is suffused with contrails, nerves, connections that run eons deep, they trail back to the very beginnings of time and space and point forward to the unmapped future; they suture then-and-now-and-next together into intricate networks of cause and effect. Does the complexity that burgeons around each fragment of experience whenever we stop to reflect on it offer any hope of redemption in terms of finding some overarching sense? When we see the mundane particular wedded to the incredible general, does it point to meanings we can grasp, or does it simply restate at another level the incomprehensibility of being? On the one hand, *the sparrowhawk kill I witnessed* can be labelled thus and left. On the other hand, it connects me to a voltage that arcs out of its containment in a bounded moment and connects to dimensions whose singular uniqueness seems to defy the grasp of metaphor.

As it happens, *the sparrowhawk kill I witnessed* took place in the same week that I was reading *The Best American Essays 2019*. As "Fitting In" took shape, Rebecca Solnit's deft identification of the key characteristics of the genre kept coming back to mind, so much so that I decided in the end to include her words as my epigraph. In part what I witnessed made me simply "want to recount things that happened." But by far the most powerful motive for writing lay in a desire to "contemplate what they mean." The fact that my contemplation offers no easy answers, is open-ended, that it shows how resistant to constraint within routine categories the things around us are once we start to think about them, perhaps explains why essaying is an ongoing art rather than some quotidian task that can be wound up with a neat conclusion.

Notes

Footnotes belong to academic writing, not to essay collections. However, it seemed appropriate to acknowledge the sources used in the Introduction, and to provide some background information for a few of the essays.

Introduction

William Blake's "To see a world in a grain of sand" is from his "Auguries of Innocence," first published in 1863, in the edition of his *Poems* edited by Dante Gabriel Rossetti. In the original poem, Blake capitalizes many of the words he uses in its most famous verse. I've not retained the capitalizations in my quote (of "World," "Sand," "Heaven," "Flower," Infinity," etc.). Phillip Lopate's "In Defense of the Miscellaneous Essay Collection" can be found in *Portrait Inside My Head: Essays* (New York: Simon & Schuster: 2014), 1–5. E. J. Levy's, "In Defense of Incoherence," is in *Occasional Papers on the Essay: Practice and Form,* in Welcome Table Press Pamphlet Series (June 2011), 14–16. Graham Good's comment is made in his preface to *The Encyclopedia of the Essay*, edited by Tracy Chevalier (London: Fitzroy Dearborn, 1997), xxi. My quote from Richard Chadbourne is taken from his brilliant article "A Puzzling Literary Genre: Comparative Views of the Essay." This appeared in *Comparative Literature Studies*, 20, no.1 (1983): 131–53.

Incidentally, I consider Phillip Lopate to be one of the patron saints of the genre. He has done much to promote its positive reception among contemporary readers. What I've said in the Introduction is not intended as a criticism of his excellent (miscellaneous) essay collection. *Portrait Inside My Head* is a delight to read.

Particle Metaphysics

This essay shares its title with a book published in the same year that my photograph of Railway Street was taken, Brigitte Falkenburg's *Particle Metaphysics*. The coincidence of titles is accidental; I only discovered Falkenburg's book after writing the essay. It should be obvious that I'm not offering the kind of critical account of subatomic reality that she elegantly provides. Fascinating though this is, I'm not interested here in exploring whether the particles of matter that physicists posit are real or fictitious entities — or if they occupy some paradoxical middle ground of existence between imagination and actuality. My concern is with the way in which the constituent parts of our experience (in this case a photograph, but it could as easily have been something else) can be read in two quite different ways. One way confines them to the ordinary physics of common sense, where things can be described, defined, labelled, and categorized in a straightforward manner. The other way reads them so that they break out of such confinements and point to much more wide-reaching perspectives (the metaphysics). My use of *particle* also deliberately taps into the word's meaning as "a crumb of consecrated bread," thus pointing to the dimension of wonder-reverence-revelation that can accompany the metaphysical dimensions of particles and the sense of near sacrality that they can — should? — engender.

Pulse

"To compile all the facts known about the bird's egg . . ." Alexis L. Romanoff and Anastasia J. Romanoff, *The Avian Egg* (New York: John Wiley, 1949), 1.

"If required on pain of death . . ." T. W. Higginson, as quoted by Romanoff and Romanoff, *The Avian Egg*, 1.

"Before hatching, the chick starts to call . . ." Desmond Nethersole-Thompson, *The Oystercatcher* (Aylesbury: Shire Publications, 1988), 14.

"The most strenuous activity in which . . ." Noble S. Proctor and Patrick J Lynch, *Manual of Ornithology* (New Haven, Conn.: Yale University Press, 1993), 189.

"Increases by more than a thousand times . . ." Ruth Bellairs and Mark Osmond, *The Atlas of Chick Development*, 3rd ed. (Oxford: Academic Press/ Elsevier, 2014), 57.

"Perform the silent industry of life . . ." Gavin Francis, *Adventures in Being Human* (London: Profile Books, 2015), 89.

"Appear in the Early Cretaceous . . ." Gareth Dyke and Gary Kaiser, eds., *Living Dinosaurs: The Evolutionary History of Modern Birds* (Oxford: Wiley-Blackwell, 2011), 5.

"There are some people who see . . ." Thomas Henry Huxley, *The Life and Letters of Thomas Henry Huxley* (London: Macmillan, 1900), 2: 437–38.

"We have to bear in mind that . . ." Max Jammer uses this comment of Albert Einstein's as the epigraph for his book *Concepts of Simultaneity from Antiquity to Einstein and Beyond* (Baltimore: Johns Hopkins University Press, 2006).

"When we try to pick out anything by itself . . ." John Muir, *My First Summer in the Sierra*, (Boston: Houghton Mifflin, 1911). The quote is from p.110 of the Sierra Club Books 1988 edition.

"And we should die of that roar . . ." George Eliot, *Middlemarch: A Study of Provincial Life* (Edinburgh: William Blackwood, Edinburgh, n.d.), 141. *Middlemarch* was first published 1871–72.

In the Stomach of a Termite

All quotes in this essay are taken from Richard Dawkins, *The Ancestor's Tale: A Pilgrimage to the Dawn of Life* (London: Weidenfeld & Nicholson, 2004).

Fitting In

My epigraph is from Rebecca Solnit's excellent introduction to *The Best American Essays 2019* (Boston and New York: Mariner Books: 2019). Ian Newton's words are taken from his *Sparrowhawk* (Calton: Poyser, 1986), which remains the best monograph on this species. Ted Hughes's "Hawk Roosting" is included in his second collection, *Lupercal* (London: Faber, 1960). The full text of the poem can easily be found online. Montaigne's reflections on movement occur at various points in his essays. I'm referring especially to what he says in Book III, "On Repentance": see Michel de Montaigne, *The Complete Works*, trans. Donald Frame, (London: Everyman's Library, 2003), 740. "On Repentance" is thought to date from 1585–88. Appropriately, given the bloodiness of this essay's point of focus, my quotes from José Ortega y Gasset and Jonathan Miller are both taken from James M. Bradbourne, ed., *Blood: Art, Power, Politics and Pathology* (Munich: Prestel, 2001), 16. J. L. Austin's thoughts on the way in which *like* constitutes our "main flexibility device by whose aid, in spite of our limited vocabulary, we can always avoid being left completely speechless," can be found in his classic of linguistic philosophy, *Sense and Sensibilia* (Oxford: Clarendon Press, 1962), 74. I'm pleased to have been able to include quotations from J. A. Baker's incomparable *The Peregrine* (London: Collins, 1967), and James Macdonald Lockhart's *Raptor: A Journey through Birds* (London: Fourth Estate, 2016). The fact that I don't mention Helen Macdonald's *H Is for Hawk* (London: Jonathan Cape, 2014) should not be read as an adverse judgment. Her book is another piece of quite brilliant raptor-inspired writing.

Acknowledgments

Writing claims time in abundance, our most precious and least renewable natural resource. I'm grateful to Jane, Lucy, and Laura for so graciously putting up with the temporal demands my books make on family life.

Parts of *Hidden Cargoes* were written while I was a Royal Literary Fund Fellow at the University of Dundee. Not only has the RLF Fellowship provided the kind of financial security writers rarely enjoy, but the way in which the scheme is operated does much to bolster a writer's sense of literary self-worth. Under the deft but light-touch leadership of Steve Cook and David Swinburne, the Fellowship offers a wonderfully supportive milieu in which to work. Steve and David have, I suspect, played a significant role in moving many books toward publication. I'm grateful for the part they've played in doing so with this one.

Versions of several of the essays in *Hidden Cargoes* have been published singly. Thank you to the *Antigonish Review, Dalhousie Review, Fourth Genre, Hotel Amerika, ISLE: Interdisciplinary Studies in Literature and Environment, Montreal Review, New Hibernia Review, Terrain.org*, and *Water~Stone Review*. I'm grateful to the editors of these journals, not only for allowing me to reprint the essays here but also for providing valuable encouragement along the way.

228

Thank you to Robert Atwan and Phillip Lopate, key figures in the resurgence of the contemporary essay, whose work has done so much to alert people to the existence and potential of this still too-often-marginalized literary genre. It means a lot to me to have their generously given endorsements of my work.

In an early communication with EastOver Press I was told: "We are all writers ourselves. Our goal is to treat you as we want to be treated." It has been a pleasure to work with a publisher that puts this ethos into practice. Thank you to Walter Robinson and his co-editors for all the time, energy, and imagination they've devoted to moving *Hidden Cargoes* from raw typescript to published book.

Some writers claim not to look at or be influenced by reviews of their work. I am not one of them. Comment from reviewers, and from ordinary readers, provides an important stimulus for thinking about what I'm doing. I find it helpful to stand back from my writing every now and then and look at it through other people's perspectives. The feedback I receive provides valuable touchstones on the long, hard route that leads from initial ideas to publication. For their assessments of previous books, I'm particularly grateful to the following reviewers: Patricia Craig, Frances Devlin-Glass, Graham Good, Kirsty Gunn, Glenn Hooper, Luci Collin Lavalle, Marion Naugrette-Fournier, David Robinson, Denis Sampson, Eoghan Smith, Sam Thompson, Rob Volmarr, and Ellen Wiles. Unpublished but no less perceptive comments have been offered by Mary Hood, Graham Johnston, Maren O. Mitchell, Maeve Nolan, Dorcas Sohn, and Andy Wainwright.